BUSINESS COMPETITION
CUSTOMER SERVICE PRODUCT
PUBLICITY WEBSITE
BRANDING REF
PROMOTION ANALYSIS PROMOT
MARKETING P
BRANDING
CUSTOMER SERVICE

THE MARKETING HANDBOOK
FOR SPORTS & FITNESS
PROFESSIONALS

NITA A. MARTIN

A&C BLACK • LONDON

Published in 2009 by A&C Black Publishers Ltd
36 Soho Square, London W1D 3QY
www.acblack.com

Copyright © Nita A. Martin 2009
ISBN 978 1 4081 1479 7

A CIP catalogue record for this book is available from the British Library.

Acknowledgements
Cover photograph © www.istockphoto.com
Illustration by Jeff Edwards
Designed by Steve Russell

This book is produced using paper that is made from wood grown in managed, sustainable forests. It is natural, renewable and recyclable. The logging and manufacturing processes conform to the environmental regulations of the country of origin.

Typeset in 9.5 on 12pt Avenir Light by Palimpsest Book Production Limited
Grangemouth, Stirlingshire

Printed and bound in Spain by GraphyCems

CONTENTS

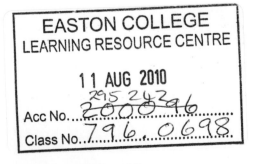

INTRODUCTION

Whether you have just started up your own coaching business or are established and looking for ways to help you grow your business, you will need to think about marketing. As a sports or fitness coach, your business could really benefit from having a structured approach in this area. Marketing is all about getting your services to the market, your target customers. In order for you to generate customers, you need to make sure that people can find out about your business. To do that, you need to know who your customers are and exactly what it is that you are offering. That is where this book comes in useful.

The Marketing Handbook for Sports & Fitness Professionals provides a structured approach to marketing that is directly aimed at sports and fitness professionals. The book is split into three parts. In the first part we take a look at:

- **The importance of marketing for sports and fitness professionals**
- **Developing your business offering**
- **Identifying your customers**
- **Understanding how your customers make purchases**
- **Focusing on your strengths and uniqueness**
- **Planning to make marketing easier**
- **Making marketing a core business activity**

At the end of this part of the book, you should have built up a really good idea about what it is that you want to market and who you want to market it to. You should also have started thinking about what your coaching programme looks like, so that you can consider what marketing you would need in order to support it. If, like many sports and fitness professionals, you work on your own, this book will help you to build an approach that will work for you personally. The objective is to create your very own tailor-made marketing plan, and part I of this book is packed with exercises, examples and templates to help you to achieve this.

The second part of this book looks specifically at a range of marketing techniques that work for sports and fitness professionals. The idea is that, now that you know what you want to market, you can pick and mix techniques from the chapters in this part of the book. The marketing technique chapters are split into entry-level, intermediate and advanced traditional options and include a chapter on electronic techniques, as shown below.

- **Pick and mix your marketing techniques**
- **Entry-level traditional marketing techniques**
- **Intermediate traditional marketing techniques**
- **Advanced traditional marketing techniques**
- **Electronic marketing techniques**

As you work through these chapters, you should identify which marketing activities you would be interested in trying out first for your business. Traditional techniques include things such as leafleting, direct mail, directory listings and developing merchandise. Electronic techniques include things such as using electronic newsletters and developing your own website.

Part III of this book looks at helping you to use all the information collected from parts I and II and pull together a marketing plan. These chapters also include exercises and templates. As well as preparing a marketing plan, you'll need to consider how you will track your progress and measure its effectiveness. You'll also need to think about what you can do about customer service to make sure that you keep the customers whom you get. The chapters in this part of the book are as follows:

- **Preparing your tailor-made marketing plan**
- **Measuring effectiveness**
- **Managing customer service**
- **The ongoing marketing process**

PART I
MARKETING BASICS

CHAPTER 1
THE IMPORTANCE
OF MARKETING FOR SPORTS
AND FITNESS PROFESSIONALS

Being successful as a sports or fitness professional requires more than just knowing your discipline inside and out. Without successful marketing, even the best professionals can struggle to get new customers and to keep their current ones. If you have never done any marketing before, the prospect can be quite daunting. You may feel that you don't know where to start or how much of your time and energy you should be devoting to such an activity. If this is the case it will divert your attention from spending time with fee-paying customers. However, if you do not put in place a process for generating new business and getting new customers and members, you may well find that your business is short lived. Running a business is all about finding customers. In order to start and later grow your business, you need to find a way of generating a steady stream of customers coming to you. This is where marketing comes in. Love it or loathe it, it can be the essential ingredient to making your coaching business a success.

For new businesses
If you are thinking about setting up a sports or fitness coaching business, start thinking about marketing before you give up your day job. Many sports and fitness professionals start up their business in their spare time and coach in the evenings and at the weekends. This can be a great way to minimise the risk of lost income to you while you get your business up and running in earnest. It is also a good way to explore and test ideas, both in terms of marketing and in terms of your business.

If you have never done any marketing or created a marketing plan before, don't worry. This book will guide you through the steps that will enable you to develop your very own marketing plan to help you get started in attracting customers. Remember that being a successful sports or fitness professional requires you to be good at business and marketing as well as at coaching. The good news is that you can learn the business and marketing skills that you need.

Good marketing should enable you to work towards creating a pipeline of new business for you. It can be quite hard work starting off in business and getting new customers in, so you always need to keep an eye out for where your next customer will be coming from. Your marketing efforts may take time to generate business for you and so you want to ensure that you are continually priming your pipeline to get new customers.

For existing businesses

If you are already running a sports or fitness coaching business and you haven't yet tried any formal marketing activities, you need to consider how you are currently getting your customers. For example, if you get them solely through referrals and word of mouth, are you confident that:

- **you are generating as many customers as you would ideally like?**
- **marketing won't bring in more business for you?**
- **your current source of customers won't dry up?**

If you are at a point where you want to see if marketing can help you to enhance and grow your business, the process in this book for developing and executing your very own marketing plan can help you. How you market can depend on what the lag time is between a potential customer finding out about you and when they actually make their first purchase. In some businesses, this can be less than a day and in others it could be several years. Creating a marketing plan that works for you will help to keep your pipeline filled and to ensure that you have fewer droughts in your business.

For example, if you are a sports coach, you may be trying to increase the number of students whom you coach during the day so that you can take your business from being part-time in the evenings and weekends to being a full-time activity allowing you to leave your other day job. Or you may be keen on finding ways to increase how much you earn while decreasing how much time you spend working.

Reasons for marketing

You need to have clearly written down the objectives that you have for your marketing plan. In this way, you can check that the activities which you are proposing directly contribute to one or more of those objectives. If those activities don't satisfy this requirement, you need to drop them and try other activities that could meet those objectives.

Have a look at exercise 1.1. It lists a number of ways in which marketing can help sports and fitness professionals. Does this list seem to cover the kinds of thing you would want your marketing to do for you? Have a go at ordering the reasons for marketing in line with what you would like to achieve from your marketing today. You may, for example, be keen on increasing your sales and your profits or you may be in urgent need of finding new customers. Your marketing priorities and objectives can change over time. This doesn't mean that you don't want to achieve all the things in the list: it just means that where you focus your efforts may change from time to time. For this reason, it can be useful to review your priorities at least every year to ensure that your planned marketing activities are in line with your marketing objectives. You can always double check that each of your marketing activities directly contributes to at least one of your marketing objectives from exercise 1.1.

Exercise 1.1: Prioritise the reasons why marketing is important in order of what you want to achieve for your sports or fitness business today.

MARKETING OBJECTIVE	YOUR PRIORITY RANKING
Maximise your profits	
Create a pipeline of new customers	
Create a repeatable process to get new customers	
Create demand for your services	
Demonstrate that you are the best choice	
Build your reputation	
Raise awareness of your business	
Minimise the effects of business famine	
Focus on delivering	

The list in exercise 1.1 is not exhaustive. You may have other reasons why you feel that you would want to do marketing. The key is to ensure that you make a note of what those are so that you can use them to provide direction for your marketing activities. How you achieve each of the objectives in exercise 1.1 will be unique to you and your business.

However, it can be helpful to have a look at how others might have interpreted those objectives and turned them into some activity that had a positive effect on their business. Have a go at exercise 1.2. It looks at the same marketing reasons; however, this time complete the exercise with how you think your most admired competitors are achieving that same objective. It should then start to give you an idea of what kinds of thing you might need to think about.

Exercise 1.2: Write down what your competitors might be doing to achieve the marketing objectives.

MARKETING OBJECTIVE	WHAT DO YOUR COMPETITORS DO?
Maximise your profits	
Create a pipeline of new customers	
Create a repeatable process to get new customers	
Create demand for your services	
Demonstrate that you are the best choice	
Build your reputation	
Raise awareness of your business	
Minimise the effects of business famine	
Focus on delivering	

The remainder of this chapter looks in detail at each of the marketing objectives shown in the exercises.

Maximise your profits

You want to have your marketing lead directly to an increase in profits. Notice that it doesn't say an increase in sales. If you increase the volume of low-profit work, you could end up being really busy and yet not have much to show for it. Therefore you want to make sure that you attract the right kind of business so that you maximise your profits while minimising your efforts.

Case study: Aerobics instructor

Take the example of an aerobics instructor running classes that are open to the public on a pay-as-you-go basis. The classes are generally low priced to attract as many people as possible. In order to increase the amount of money that she makes, the instructor increases the number of sessions that she runs by doing classes on another two weekday evenings.

Although her takings have gone up, her overall profit hasn't increased by that much. This is especially unfortunate when you take into account that she has sacrificed another two evenings of her week. This is because she has now increased her costs, namely venue hire and travel to and from the venue. If she had focused on increasing the number of people attending the classes that she was already running, her costs would have remained unchanged and all the extra sales would have converted directly into a corresponding profit.

Create a pipeline of new customers

If you can guarantee that the customers whom you already have will stay with you forever, and that they generate enough business for you to never want to grow your sales any further, then you won't need to worry about acquiring new ones. However, this is almost never the case for any business, and the sports and fitness industry is no different.

New customers are the lifeline of all businesses. While you are working with your current customers, you always need to be active in searching for new ones. In this way, hopefully, you minimise the effect of customers' leaving you, as you are constantly replenishing your customer base. In order to always have new customers regularly coming in to your business, you need to direct your marketing activities in a way which delivers that goal for you.

Potential customers may go through a staged process before they decide to buy from you. This could include their becoming aware of your business, finding out more about it, perhaps trialling a product and then evaluating their interaction with you and the quality of their purchase. All of these stages take time and you will need to have some understanding of how customers buy from you and what the relevant stages are for your business. In this way, you can make sure that you have potential customers at every stage of this process, all the time, so that there can be a steady delivery of new customers. If you don't prime your pipeline, it can take a while to start generating new business, and all the while you could be left cold without any sales at all. Even if you advertise your business today, customers may still take a year before they actually come to you. Sometimes the time lag, between somebody's becoming aware of your business and when they actually do some business with you, can be of the order of years. So if you start looking for new customers exactly when you urgently need them, it won't change the timescales of the buying process that people go through. You will just have to hope that you are still around when they are finally ready to try out your services.

Case study: Gym instructor

A gym instructor was really successful and had a good number of clients whom he regularly coached. A new manager at the fitness centre where he worked was appointed and was tasked with reducing the costs of the centre. The manager decided to cut back on the posters and leaflets that they were regularly having printed and distributed. It took the gym instructor a while to notice, but slowly he started to lose customers and he didn't seem to have any new ones arriving. Only then did the gym instructor realise that his services were no longer being promoted and that he would have to do something by himself to get the word out. However, he had never done any marketing before and so it took him some time to organise some leaflets of his own that he could distribute through the fitness centre. In the meantime, he continued to lose customers and see his business decline. It was almost three months before the gym instructor started to reap the benefit of his work on the leaflets. If your pipeline isn't full of potential customers, you can very rapidly start to see you business suffer.

Create a repeatable process to get new customers

Getting new customers can be really hard work. Wouldn't it be great to have a simple process which you could follow that yielded a steady stream of new customers? That is exactly what successful marketing should do you for you. The point of putting together a marketing plan in advance of actually getting stuck into marketing activities, as and when you feel you are running out of customers, is that having a well-thought-out process which you have tried and can build on means that you can make marketing more of a natural process which is easy to follow. You need to be marketing all the time, and so you need to find a way that works consistently for you, as well as being one that you can keep repeating. This will enable you to spend the majority of your time and energy on actually delivering the work that comes in without continually having to think about how to do your marketing.

Case study: Badminton coach

Take the example of a badminton coach who runs an eight-week course every quarter. He has a regular timetable of courses and each year he runs a similar programme. He promotes his courses in leaflets, in magazines and on his website at least one whole year in advance of the course start date. Since he has a programme of courses in place, he follows the same marketing activities each quarter to generate new clients. These include leaflets and adverts in school magazines to attract his target market.

Because the courses are regular and his services have a familiar presence in the community, he builds up a reputation and awareness of his business. In this way, when someone thinks about needing badminton coaching, they look for his details first. When he asks his customers how and when they found out about him, it turns out that it was his marketing efforts from a year or more ago that have resulted in a sale today. The fact that his marketing programme is regular and that he can try new things out each year, in addition to doing what he already knows works, means that he is always building his business proactively and keeping his pipeline filled with potential customers.

Create demand for your services

In an ideal world, wouldn't it be great to have the problem of too many customers and the ones who you already have always looking for more things that they can buy from you? This would be an enviable position indeed. In fact, it is a perfectly possible position for a sports or fitness professional to be in – if, that is, you work on creating the desire and demand for your services.

If you are not sure as to what more you could do or try for your customers, the best way to find out is to ask them. Sometimes you will get ideas from them that just don't work. But you may be able to think of ways that you can modify these ideas to give them the best chance of success. Also, showing that you take people's feedback seriously and that you are willing to act quickly and positively based on their comments will strengthen their relationship with you.

Case study: Badminton coach

Taking the example of the badminton coach again, on talking to the students who attend his courses, he may find that some of them ask him whether he does personal training. He explains that he does not do so at the moment. However, this could certainly be something that he could try quite easily. He might be worried about how he would make sure that he can afford to teach one person when there is nobody else with whom to spread the cost of the facilities hire. On looking into it further, he works out that he would need to charge quite a bit more for providing this service. But since he is providing a bespoke, higher-quality coaching service, he feels that he can justify the higher price that people would have to pay to receive personal training. He tests his new pricing model on the students who asked him and adjusts it as appropriate to make sure that he can come to some form of arrangement that suits both parties.

You need to be able to take feedback, both formal and informal, positive and negative, from all around you to develop your products and services in a way that builds the demand for what you are offering.

Demonstrate that you are the best choice

Once you understand what your competitors are doing and you have pulled together ideas of which services you wish to provide, you will need to find some way of differentiating yourself and attracting customers to your business. You need to be aware of your competition and, more importantly, of the uniqueness of your own business.

Can you describe in no more than a couple of sentences what you do and why you are the best choice for it? If you were meeting some new people and they asked you what you did, would you be able to describe it in a way that they could understand? Your message needs to be simple and yet effective. It needs to be focused so that it can direct all of your efforts to achieving your business goal. As you develop ideas for your business and how you will go about marketing it, it may be helpful to think about what you want your business to look like in the future. This can sometimes help to focus your thoughts on what you should do.

Have a go at exercise 1.3. You need to describe your business in no more than three sentences, making sure that you are clear about what it is that you do. Also add some kind of hook that will help people remember what you said; for example, you could mention something that is unique about the way that you approach your coaching.

Exercise 1.3: Describe your business in no more than three sentences. You should say clearly what you do and what is unique about your business.

1.
2.
3.

Case study: Yoga instructor

A yoga instructor who focuses on relaxation and breathing techniques may describe his business as follows.

- I teach yoga to adults who are looking for ways to relax and get away from everyday stresses.
- I focus on the development and control of breathing methods.
- I have learned these techniques through many years of training with yoga masters in India.

In these few short sentences, he has demonstrated what he does, his focus and the unique experience that he brings to his teaching. Remember, this isn't a sales pitch. It is a way to help you to focus on what your business is about. If you don't have a clear picture in your head, it can be difficult for you to be focused on your marketing efforts or your business development.

Build your reputation

Reputation is not just something that you build with new or potential customers. It is something that you should also work on with your existing clientele. There is nothing wrong in reminding your current customers of why they are doing business with you. If you can keep demonstrating the value and quality of your service, you stand the best chance of retaining your current customers as well as finding new ones. For example, you can build your reputation by:

- developing your brand
- having value-added additional services
- developing intellectual assets (e.g. here it refers to creating products such as books and videos)
- improving the quality of your services
- giving outstanding customer service
- gaining further experience and qualifications

Have a go at exercise 1.4. Can you think of ways in which you could build your reputation in various areas for your coaching business? Don't worry if you can't think of something to put in each box at this stage.

Exercise 1.4: Write down your ideas for what you could do to build your reputation.

OBJECTIVE	YOUR IDEAS
Developing your brand	
Having value-added additional services	
Developing intellectual assets	
Improving the quality of your services	
Giving outstanding customer service	
Gaining further experience and qualifications	

Case study: Martial arts instructor

Martial arts tend to have syllabuses and grading systems associated with them. Students work their way through each of the levels by regular training and examination. The instructor could build his reputation by providing information sheets of what is required for each grading and making these readily available to his students. In addition, to make new students welcome to his school, he could create beginner induction leaflets which answer the most frequently asked questions that beginners have.

Raise awareness of your business

How are people going to find out that your business exists at all? There may be many people out there who would benefit from your services. You might estimate that the market for your business is quite large, but how will you reach it? The very first stage of getting people to buy from you is to make them aware that you exist. You must get your business out in front of the people whom you are targeting, and you will need to be open to trying many different ways in which to achieve this.

Case study: Unusual sports

If your sport is less mainstream, you could get involved in taking part in local events and giving demonstrations for free so that you gain exposure and build awareness of your sport and your coaching business. Finding ways in which to let potential students have a go at your sport is also a great means of generating interest in it.

Minimise the effects of business famine

You can be hit by business famine if you don't work on keeping your pipeline filled. There are also other things that could result in business famine unless you take steps to minimise their effects. Sports and fitness businesses tend to be quite strongly affected by seasonal trends. For example, in January you may get an influx of new students as people make new-year resolutions to get fit. You may also get an influx at the same time as the new school year starts. However, you may find that summers and other school holidays are particularly quiet for most of your coaching business.

Drumming up business during naturally quiet times can take more creativity and effort than at other times. If you persevere, however, you may find that your efforts will pay off.

Case study: Sports coaches working in schools

If you coach a sport in a school, you may have the problem of not having any business during the school holidays. One way to combat this might be to set up intensive week-long training holiday camps. If this does not work, you could even try teaming up with other sports coaches and putting together a multi-sports programme for the school holidays. In this, children could come along and try out a variety of sports, including yours, and the focus is then much more on having fun and also getting exposure to lots of new sports that would otherwise be quite difficult for parents to arrange.

Focus on delivering

If you know that you have a reliable marketing plan which ensures that you have a steady stream of new customers, you can manage your marketing with little effort and still enjoy great results. This will allow you to focus on delivering to your customers and providing excellent customer service. This is the ideal case. When you get to this stage, you will still have to review your marketing plan and make time to try out new things. However, it is much easier once you know that you have some techniques in the bag that certainly do work. You will get to this stage only by putting in the work upfront in developing and fine tuning your marketing plan and efforts on an ongoing basis.

Case study: Aerobics instructor

An aerobics instructor used to promote her business in such a way that she welcomed beginners to start at any time. However, she discovered that people found this arrangement uncomfortable because they wanted to join when there were other beginners there also, as otherwise they felt lost and like the only person there who didn't know what was going on. From the instructor's viewpoint, when new students turned up on an ad hoc basis, she found that she had to tone down her class each time, which in turn affected the quality of the class for more established students.

Her solution was to try having a number of dedicated slots each month where she would promote the business as accepting beginners. She noticed that more people joined and they were happier with the class, as the induction was far smoother. It was also easier for her to teach and the more established students found that the lessons were less disturbed. Everybody won in this way.

CHAPTER 2
DEVELOPING YOUR BUSINESS OFFERING

Before you can start marketing your business, you need to be clear about exactly what your business is. This means that you should have a clear idea about things such as what coaching and products you offer, what your pricing structure is, where you will be working from, whether you need to hire venues, and what times you will be available for providing your services. The more you know and the better structured your offering is, the easier it will be for you to communicate clearly with your customers as well as market your business. How many of the questions in exercise 2.1 can you already answer?

Exercise 2.1: Answer the following questions on how well you understand your business offering.

• **What is your business?**
• **Who are your competitors?**
• **What is your brand and how are you using it?**
• **What range of coaching services do you offer?**
• **What range of products do you offer that complement your services?**
• **How do your services and products work together?**

- **How do you make use of cross-selling opportunities?**

- **What is your strategy for promoting each service and product?**

- **Where will you be working from and does it meet your business needs?**

About your business

In chapter 1 we did the exercise of describing your business in a few short and simple sentences. Now you need to build on that so that you can be clear about the messages and information you should include in your marketing materials. Without the right level of detail available, it can be difficult to figure out exactly what you are going to say about your business or your services. If you don't know what to say, it may be hard to make a start on finding how to communicate in a way that attracts customers to you. Start by defining what you will be doing. As a sports or fitness professional you may be working on your own as a:

- **fitness instructor**
- **gym instructor**
- **personal trainer**
- **sports coach**

Or you may be working as part of an organisation, such as a:

- **fitness centre**
- **health spa**
- **sports association**
- **sports club or school**
- **specialised sports school, for example a tennis academy**

You need to be clear about exactly what you are planning to coach and whether you will be doing that completely on your own or will be working through an organisation. If you are working on your own, will you be doing this as a full-time or part-time job? If you are responsible for marketing in an organisation, you also need to be clear on how much time you will be able to devote to marketing efforts, as that may not be your only role. Regardless of whether you are working for an amateur organisation or a professional organisation, marketing can help you to reach new customers or new members and also to retain existing ones. If you have set up in business casually through contacts who have referred business to you, you may not have thought much more about actually marketing yourself or your services. However, if you are looking to grow your business, marketing can provide you with the structure to start behaving in a more businesslike way that will enable you to grow your activities in a systematic manner.

A good place to start planning what marketing you need is by thinking about exactly what your business, product or service is. Exercise 2.2 can be used to help you get started in that. This will give you an indication of where you are today with your business. It can also help to highlight areas that you wish to develop. For example, you could complete a second copy of this template with the vision of how you would like to be able to describe your business in the future. Your marketing plan will then need to build the bridge to get you from where you are today to where you want to be in the future. This can form the vision for your business.

Exercise 2.2: Review the status of your business, product or service by answering the following questions.

QUESTION	YOUR ANSWERS
1. What is the name of your business?	
2. Do you have a logo or branding concept?	
3. How do you use branding on your products and services?	
4. What is the geographic scope of your business?	
5. What is the demographic scope of your business?	
6. What would you like your business to look like when it is successful?	

QUESTION	YOUR ANSWERS
7. How many customers do you already have?	
8. How do you plan to accommodate new customers?	
9. Are you aware of what your competition is doing?	

To be able to promote your business effectively, you must be clear on where you will be working from. This is especially true if you are going into business by yourself. Your training location or gym where you offer fitness sessions will need to be booked or available to you so that you can make the location known on your promotional materials. People will also need to know how to get in touch with you.

About your competitors

If you are going to set up in business, it can be useful to see what the competition is like. It can help you to think about:

- **your pricing**
- **what services and products you might offer**
- **where and how you could promote your business**

You don't necessarily need to do, or even avoid, exactly what the competition is doing. You can use this information to give you a starting point to build from. You may find that there are lots of people offering coaching services of the type that you are looking to offer. You should not necessarily let this put you off. Your competitors may even eventually form sources of new clients for you in the future. In fact, if you can create a sustainable business model and make sure that you are reliable and are going to be around for some time, the eventual closure or relocation of your current competitors could provide a natural source of new clients for you. Sometimes your services may be more appropriate or your location and pricing more favourable. Sometimes people know that they like something and want to try a new trainer to see how they get on. Perhaps they feel that they have outgrown their current trainer. You should give people the opportunity to try your coaching and decide for themselves.

You can even look to offer your services at a location where there are already similar coaches working, as long as you differentiate yourself, for example by offering sessions at different times or to a different demographic. This way you still have a good chance of winning new customers. When people are starting out in training, they may well be happy to try out a number of different trainers until they finally settle on one. You need to be aware of who your competitors are and ensure that you can demonstrate how you differentiate yourself from them. There can be both direct and indirect competitors to your business.

Case study: Direct competition for a fitness instructor

If you are a fitness instructor, direct competition could be fellow instructors who offer very similar services to yours and operate within either the same fitness centre or the same geographic region.

Case study: Indirect competition for a fitness instructor

Take the following example of indirect competition. If you are a fitness instructor, you may also be competing for your customers' time spent on activities that don't involve a personal trainer. For example, potential customers might spend time working out in the gym, swimming or jogging. All of these activities can potentially attract the same group of customers away from your business and so they are all some form of competition for you to consider.

Have a go at the questions in exercise 2.3, which aims to get you thinking about both your direct and your indirect competition.

Exercise 2.3: Complete the following to see how well you know your competition.

DIRECT COMPETITORS	YOUR ANSWERS
1. How many coaches in your local area are running a business similar to yours?	
2. How many coaches in the wider region are running a business similar to yours?	
3. Whom do you consider the most successful of your competitors?	
4. Do you have an idea of what makes them successful and is that something you can learn from and apply to your business?	

INDIRECT COMPETITORS	YOUR ANSWERS
5. What other businesses attract the types of customer whom you are targeting? For example, are you competing with the cinema and restaurants?	
6. Are there other types of sports and fitness training that are likely to appeal to the same group of people?	
7. Taking the most successful of these, is there anything that you can learn from them and apply to your business?	

Knowledge of your competition can help you to think about what you can do that would make you better than them and how you can differentiate yourself from them. In the case study of the fitness instructor, even though he may work in the same centre or region as you, it doesn't mean that your business will automatically be a failure just because you are facing the competition from a standing start. Sometimes your competition can be an excellent source of new business. Their customers might come to you for a number of reasons, including:

- **They are interested in the service that your competition is providing but they don't like that person and so they are looking for another provider of the same type of service.**
- **They are looking for someone new to continue their training with following the closure of your competition's business.**
- **They feel that they have outgrown what they can learn or what they can gain from your competition.**
- **They believe that the location where you are based, or the training timetable which you offer, suits them much better.**

There can be numerous reasons why people may come to you from competitors and so it can be worthwhile having a process for taking them in and making them feel comfortable, even if they do something slightly differently from the way that you would have taught it. Have a go at exercise 2.4 to gain a better understanding of your competitors; perhaps use copies of the template to fill in a separate page for each one of them.

Exercise 2.4: For each of the four categories, list the attributes of your chosen competitor.

CATEGORY	ATTRIBUTES
Strengths	
Weaknesses	
Opportunities	
Threats	

About your brand

Whether you actively create a brand for your business using fancy graphics and putting lots of thought into your name, or just run your business using your own name, you will still have a brand. Whatever branding method or strategy you want to use, it can pay dividends to stick to it and develop it over time, as it can work towards building your reputation, enhancing your business identity and possibly forming part of your intellectual assets should you ever wish to franchise or sell your business. In exercise 2.5, indicate if you already have branding for the listed items.

Exercise 2.5: Tick the boxes for the items on which you currently put your branding.

BRANDING USE	TICK IF ALREADY IN PLACE
1. Promotional materials	
2. Website	
3. Application or other forms	
4. Invoices	

BRANDING USE	TICK IF ALREADY IN PLACE
5. Clothing that you use for your business	
6. Business card	
7. Products	
8. Merchandise	
9. Car or van	

Branding can take the form of a logo or a particular use of colour, and may include punchlines as well as design ideas. Branding can be used to join all of your marketing efforts together and also to create an identifiable image for you in your community. Now have a go at exercise 2.6 and write down any ideas that you have for the branding of your business.

Exercise 2.6: Make a list of your branding ideas.

1.
2.
3.
4.
5.
6.

Your range of coaching services

Once you have an overall idea of what your business is about, you should then make sure that you clearly understand the services that you offer, as these are what people will be purchasing from you. Make a list of your services in exercise 2.7. If you have a really large repertoire, you should group your products and services so that you can think about how to market to people interested in those groups.

Exercise 2.7: List all the products and services that you offer.

1.
2.
3.
4.
5.
6.
7.
8.

Now, looking at your list, think about a customer considering purchasing from you. Does your list cater for:

- **Adults?**
- **Children?**
- **Families?**
- **Different times and locations?**
- **Different types of session based on ability?**
- **Different types of session based on different levels of interest?**
- **Different teaching objectives?**
- **Individual coaching?**
- **Smaller groups or more focused coaching?**

Is there a range of services or products from which they can select on the basis of their budget or the amount of risk they are willing to take in trying something new? Most people prefer to buy from people whom they know and trust. Given this, if you want to sell to people whom you don't already know, you will need to work on building that element of trust and reliability so that they feel comfortable purchasing from you. When somebody tries out your business for the first time, they are taking a risk. If you can find ways in which to make the risk lower, you may find that more people are willing to give it a go, and then at least you have a chance to sell some more to them later. Otherwise, people may not even try your coaching in the first place.

Tempting people to try your services

This doesn't necessarily just boil down to lowering your prices, although that is one method you can try. Having an introductory offer or service can help to reduce the barrier to getting new customers. Examples include:

- Taster sessions
- Introductory sessions
- Demonstrations
- Short-term trials
- Weekend or holiday camps

Taster sessions

Taster sessions are specific sessions that you run for people to come along to try your coaching, your sport or your training. There is no pressure to get people to sign up for membership or to even come along to more sessions. The session isn't just about training – it is a proper introduction to your training or sport. This means that it also includes some form of background and description about the training, what the benefits are and how people who are interested can find out more or join in later. There should also be a proper opportunity for people to ask questions and to give feedback.

Introductory sessions

These are slightly different to taster sessions in that they are more like the very first session that someone would do if they intend to carry on training. So this lesson may be far more focused on actually developing some basic skills that will make future lessons easier for the student.

Demonstrations

You may arrange these completely separately from your normal coaching. This is perhaps where you are trying to show all the exciting things that your training has to offer. A demonstration is meant to excite and inspire people about your training. Is there some feature of your training that people love to watch? Is there a set piece that you could create which would be awe inspiring? Demonstrations should be fun and have the ability to make people feel motivated into getting involved themselves.

Short-term trials

You could consider offering a series of lessons for free or at a reduced price in order to attract new students. This short-term trial would enable them to see what it would be like to train with you, without having to make a significant investment in equipment or membership fees. You should remember to take away as many of the barriers as you can to people trying out your training.

Weekend or holiday camps

Training camps can be an excellent means of attracting people to your business. They are useful in a number of different ways in that they:

- **allow time-poor people to try something new**
- **keep your business busy during holiday periods**
- **attract people to your business who may not otherwise try your training**

You should organise your course to fit into the period allowed and not necessarily use the same format as you always do. If you run weekly classes, remember that a holiday camp is something quite different. You may need to think carefully about the pace and content of your teaching to make it appropriate both for the audience and for such an intensive course. You will have to take into account giving your students rest periods and ensuring that your sessions work well together so that you don't overexert your students in a short burst of intensive training.

If you had only one item on your service list, or maybe even just a couple, have a rethink using the information above as inspiration and see if there is anything else that you could add to your coaching list, or a better way of grouping your services so that you could attract more customers. Write this down in exercise 2.8, and remember that it is better not to have a one-size-fits-all approach.

Exercise 2.8: Prepare a list of the services which you could offer that could grow your client base or even encourage existing customers to try something new with you.

1.
2.

3.	
4.	
5.	
6.	
7.	
8.	

Having a range of products that complement your services

Now that you have thought about the service or services which you will offer, it is worth considering whether there are products which you could offer that would complement your sports or fitness business. For example, if you are a sports coach, is there a uniform that your students could purchase from you? If so, you could look into finding a wholesale supplier for uniforms and then offer them to your students at retail price. Have a look at the following list of things that you could consider as complementary products to your services:

- Special clothing or equipment required for your sport or fitness programme, for example martial arts uniforms, riding outfits, rackets or trainers
- Books or DVDs that your programme follows which you could purchase wholesale
- Supplementary fitness equipment that you could recommend, for example weights, training mats or a Swiss ball
- Music that you could recommend to your customers to train to

Now create your own list of complementary products in exercise 2.9.

Exercise 2.9: Make a list below of products that you could offer to supplement your services.

1.
2.
3.
4.
5.
6.
7.
8.

These products won't necessarily be large income generators but, if you can offer them easily, you will be adding value to the service that you are providing to your customers. It may even form a handy side-income stream for you that you may be able to build on in the future. It will help you to start thinking more widely about products that you could offer and make you more comfortable with the concept of trying out new ideas. Then, if they don't work, you just don't do them again. Remember that you don't necessarily need to keep items in stock. You could offer merchandise for sale and then order it in when you receive an order from your customers. In this way, you are minimising your financial exposure.

Having a mix of services and products that work together

Now that you have pulled together your ideas about which services and products you will be offering, you need to think next about how you can

perhaps package them into bundles to make them easier for y
build up an idea of exactly when you should suggest a certain
or product in your range. There are many ways in which you c
about how your products work together. Perhaps certain bits o
complement certain types of training and other pieces of equi
more relevant to other types of training.

Case study: Sports instructor

Imagine that you are a sports instructor. When a new student joins, you want to give them time to see whether they like both the sport and your business. Once they have settled in and have decided to become regular students, you may want to suggest to them, say after five training sessions, that maybe they would like to consider purchasing some appropriate sports equipment which is required for the sport. This could be, for instance, a racket, a uniform or special footwear. Once they have been training with you for about three months, it might be an appropriate time to suggest some kind of supplementary training book, so that they could read up on the details of the activity you are coaching. A year into the training might be about the right time to see whether they would be interested in some of your premium services such as one-to-one tuition.

In this way, you haven't tried to sell the student everything in one go or right at the start of your relationship. You have suggested products that are appropriate for them and at a time when it would make sense to consider buying them. You need to believe in the value that you are offering, otherwise it will be difficult for you to convince people to buy from you.

Identifying cross-selling opportunities

It can be worthwhile thinking about how your products and services complement one another. Having a clear cross-sell tactic in place can make it easier for you to upgrade your client or to naturally lead on to another sale. If you create a mix of products and services that work well together, you will find it far easier to generate more revenue from the clients whom you already have.

When you have new clients come along, is there a range of products that can support them at this stage? And as they develop or progress as your clients, are there relevant products and services that you can offer them to support their transition? A well-thought-out product and service mix can make it much easier to sell to the people who already know you and trust you as a reliable supplier. Have a go at exercise 2.10 and see whether you can think of products that would work well with the range of training that you do.

Exercise 2.10: Make a list of the services that you offer and then write next to it any ideas that you have for products and services that would be natural cross-sell opportunities.

SERVICE	FOLLOW-ON PRODUCTS AND SERVICES
1.	
2.	
3.	
4.	
5.	
6.	
7.	
8.	
9.	
10.	

Having a strategy for promoting each service and product

Now that you have thought through which services and products you will offer and how they will work together, you can start considering how you will promote each one. Make a note of this in exercise 2.11.

Exercise 2.11: List all of your services and products and how you are planning to promote each one.

SERVICES AND PRODUCTS	PROMOTION STRATEGY

Once you have completed the exercise, you should hopefully have a feel for where there might be weaknesses in how well you are promoting each of your items. As you work your way through this book and on to part III about developing your marketing plan, you should review exercise 2.11 again and check that you are making the most of the promotional activities that you have decided to try.

CHAPTER 3
IDENTIFYING
YOUR CUSTOMERS

Do you have a clear picture in your mind of who your customers are? Are you providing services only to adults or do you also coach children? Are your end user and your customer one and the same? For example, do you teach children in schools, and is it the schools that are buying in your services? Why are they buying from you? Why are they looking for the product or service that you provide? Is it the end user or the customer who benefits? You need to be clear about your interaction with the users of your coaching service and the difference between them and the person or organisation that actually authorises or purchases your services.

As you can see from these questions, this information can help you to think about who it is that you are aiming your marketing towards. Sometimes it will be the actual user, but it may also be somebody else. You may even need to be able to market successfully to two separate groups in order to get the business that you are after. For example, if you teach football or cricket to children, it is both the children and the parents who are the target audience for your marketing efforts.

When you are thinking about who your customers are, this question can have many aspects to it that can be helpful in figuring out what would be the best marketing approach for your business. In exercise 3.1, how many of the questions have you thought about and have some answers to?

Exercise 3.1: How well do you know your customers or your target customers? Tick the questions below that you have thought about and have some answers to.

QUESTION	TICK BOX
1. How do your customers vary between your products and services?	
2. Why do they buy?	
3. Who does the buying and who benefits from the purchase?	
4. Which of your services, products and customers are the most profitable?	

continued

QUESTION	TICK BOX
5. What is the demographic of your customers?	
6. What is the geographic location of your customers?	
7. Can you summarise your target market?	

The list of questions in the exercise is not definitive. The idea is to get you to start thinking about the right types of question to help you to better understand your customers. You can then use this information to perhaps refine your service and product range as well as improve the quality and targeting of your marketing. You need to be really clear what you will be marketing and to whom you will be marketing it. Once you have a clear idea of who your customers are, you can start thinking about the ways in which you might reach people of that type.

Understanding how your customers vary between your products and services

If you are already in business, have you thought about how your customers vary between each of your products and services? It may be that you have some services that appeal to all of your customers and some that appeal only to a much smaller selection. Do you run group classes and also offer personal training? Do you find that the profile of the customers differs between the former and the latter? Do group customers often migrate to personal training or the other way around?

Or you might have services that appeal to businesses and others that appeal to individuals. For example, if you are a fitness instructor running your own classes, you may find that your personal training services are also bought in by sports, fitness and health centres that are looking to be able to provide the types of service through their centres that you offer. Schools and holiday camps are other examples where your personal training or group training services may be bought in. Once you understand who your customers are and which services appeal to whom, this can help you to better understand your target market and make the most of directing your marketing activities towards it.

For each product and service that you offer, you also need to consider who your customers are. This should hopefully also help you to start thinking about how your services might appeal to other types of customer, for example organisations that need sports and fitness professionals.

Identifying why they buy

Have you considered why people would buy from you? Do you offer something that nobody else does? Is it an innovative approach to supplying fitness training that you are the first to exploit? Have you built up a brand or reputation that can attract people to you? Why is it that they are interested in your services? For example, were they looking for:

- **a fun way to get fit?**
- **the right level of group classes where they didn't feel out of their depth?**
- **the right kind of person who could motivate them to train?**
- **the individual attention of an instructor, and you offer that option?**
- **some material or training method that you cover but nobody else does?**
- **a friendly training environment?**
- **inspiration, motivation and enthusiasm that they hadn't found elsewhere?**

There can be many reasons why people decide to look into training and why they might pick you in particular. Each individual may have their own reasons, but some themes or patterns may emerge that can help you better understand what attracts people to your business. Once you have discovered that, you can take more decisive action to ensure that you make the most of your strengths to grow your business.

Identifying who does the buying and who benefits from the purchase

Another thing to be aware of is whether the person who is buying your services is the same person as the one who will be benefiting from them. It is not always a straightforward case that they are one and the same. If you teach children, it might be that it is the parents who want them to train and that they are responsible for selecting you. Alternatively, it may be that a fitness centre is purchasing your services and that, although your clients benefit from your training, it will be the fitness centre that will benefit from the provision of your services.

Being clear about who the key individuals are in the buying and benefiting process will help you to be clear in your mind about where you need to focus your customer service efforts. Even if you are an excellent instructor and your students really enjoy training with you, unless the organisation that hired you is also aware of your success and the benefits that you are bringing, you may not be able to build a sustainable relationship with the right people. Therefore, you must be clear about how many parties you need to market to and provide good customer service to.

Knowing which of your services, products and customers are the most profitable

Of your range of services and products, are you aware of which ones are the most profitable? Or do you have particular services and products that attract the kinds of customer who upgrade to more profitable services? You need to know which ones in your service range are the most profitable and how you get customers to buy them. This can then help you to ensure that you put most of your marketing efforts into trying to get the most profitable business. Understanding the value to you of each of the products and services will help you to manage your range. For example:

- **Do they build your reputation?**
- **Do they help to attract the right kinds of customer?**
- **Do they help you to keep the right kinds of customer?**
- **Are you aware of which of your services are most important to your business?**

If your low-profit products lead customers to your high-profit products, you cannot focus on marketing just your high-end products at the expense of your low-end ones. You will need to ensure you thoroughly understand how everything in your range works together to create a successful business. If you have only one type of service and nothing else that you could offer your customers, this may encourage you to think about what you could offer that could mean that your business also had the ability to upgrade customers to high-profit products.

Many businesses have started to offer value or budget ranges of products that attract many customers and also lead to the sales of higher-margin products. The same tactic can be used by sports and fitness professionals. A simple example is that of offering group classes that are low cost and attract many customers to whom you could offer premium services such as one-to-one coaching. Many of your customers may not be interested in such an upgrade, but some might and that could be enough to make it worth your while offering such an additional service.

Having thought about how your customers come to buy, have a go at exercise 3.2 and see whether you now have a better idea of the answers and how you can use them to help you focus your marketing.

Exercise 3.2: List your services and products and answer the questions about who buys from you.

LIST YOUR PRODUCTS AND SERVICES	WHY DO THEY BUY?	WHO MAKES THE DECISION TO PURCHASE?	WHO BENEFITS FROM THE PURCHASE?	HOW PROFITABLE IS THIS ITEM?

The demographic of your customers

Have you thought about whether your target customers will be adults or children? If they are adults, are you aiming specifically at men or at women? If they are children, is there a particular age group that you are targeting? Are your customers likely to be single or married? Are they likely to have children? What kind of income range do you suspect your customers will fall into and does this vary between the services that you offer?

A lot of sports and fitness professionals may start off hoping to attract every single kind of customer to their business. But it can be very difficult to market to such a broad range when you are starting out. If you have a particular customer segment that you feel is likely to be the main type of customer, then that can help you to focus your marketing in ways that will appeal strongly to that demographic. If you try to make it accessible to one and all, you may just end up alienating everybody.

This is not to say that you should turn away customers who don't fit into the demographic that you have defined. In fact, the best thing to do is to start off with some idea of your target market and then, as your business develops and you get more customers, you can review whether your initial ideas and assumptions were correct or whether you need to modify and redefine your target market.

The idea of identifying the demographic of your customers is to help you to target your marketing efforts. Marketing can take time, money and effort and so you want to make sure that you are making the most of your resources. Knowing the demographic that you are targeting for your marketing efforts will help you to make decisions about where to market your services and about the content of your marketing, and even to identify, say, the right newspapers and magazines that you may want to consider advertising through to market your business.

The location of your customers

A sports or fitness business is likely to be heavily location dependent. Most people will want to look for somewhere to train near where they live or work. Sometimes, if they are more serious about their sport or fitness training, they are likely to be happy to go further afield to get what they are looking for. However, for the majority of sports and fitness businesses, location will be all-important to the success of their business.

If you are expecting people to travel quite far to train with you, then you will need to find ways to provide a unique experience that makes them continue to invest the effort to come to your business and not to go somewhere else more convenient. The other thing to bear in mind is that people might be willing to travel further, or you can reach people further away, depending on the products and services that you offer. Strong brand identity, marketing and a solid service and product range can help to attract customers from further afield. Let's take the extreme case of a personal trainer who wants to serve customers globally. Now that may seem like quite a challenge; however, it is possible as long as they can come up with innovative ways of reaching new customers.

Case study: Personal trainer

Take the case of a fitness instructor who provides personal training. He might be happy to teach locally and maybe even commute a short distance to teach, but how could he reach customers who are further away or attract them to come to him? One of the ways is to build up an excellent reputation and to develop intellectual assets and a product range that can serve people remotely. Examples of this could include:

- **Books, DVDs and perhaps even training music to enable him to reach a global market**
- **A clothing range that is branded with the business and can be sold through retail outlets as well as his own website**
- **His own branded supplements range or nutritional advice and recipes**
- **Perhaps even online services that can be managed and fulfilled wholly through the website**

From the examples given in the personal trainer case study, you will see that there can be many ways to reach different sets of customers: it all depends on the range of products and services that you create. In order to serve customers further afield, you may need to come up with new ideas about what would be most appropriate and feasible for you to sell.

Summarising your target market

Now you should be building up a pretty good idea about your customers, or at least be thinking about how to determine who your customers are and how you can market to reach them. Now think about your customers more broadly to see if you can identify anything else that could help you to reach them. Questions such as those listed below may help you to better understand your customers:

- **Do they understand the health benefits from taking part in sports and fitness activities?**

- Do they have a genuine childhood interest in your activity?
- Are they looking to compete locally, regionally, nationally or even internationally?
- Are they training just to keep fit and active?
- Are they training just for fun and are not that interested in working hard in their training?
- Do they have a dislike for team sports and so are attracted to activities that better suit individuals?
- Do they have access to the Internet and are they happy to communicate with you and purchase from you online?
- Have there been recent TV or movie successes that have inspired people to try your activity?

The answers to these questions can help you to decide what your marketing messages will be and what design or approach may work best with your customers. In exercise 3.3, fill in the customer profile for each of your services and products.

One size does not fit all

Having gone to all this effort to define your target market, remember that you should not take a one-size-fits-all approach. People are individuals and different things about your business will attract them to you. The best thing that you can do is offer them a well-thought-out product and service range and then give them outstanding customer service. Never underestimate the ability of excellent customer service to win you customer loyalty.

Exercise 3.3: List your services and products and answer the questions about your customer profile. This will help you to summarise who your target market is for each item in your list.

LIST YOUR PRODUCTS AND SERVICES	WHAT IS THE DEMOGRAPHIC OF YOUR CUSTOMERS?	WHAT IS THE GEOGRAPHIC LOCATION OF YOUR CUSTOMERS?	WHAT IS THEIR BACKGROUND?	WHAT IS THEIR MOTIVATION TO TRAIN?	SUMMARISE YOUR TARGET MARKET

CHAPTER 4
UNDERSTANDING HOW YOUR CUSTOMERS MAKE PURCHASES

Some professionals may just have a single service that they offer and some may have many. For each item or group, you need to understand the buying process. In this way, you can identify on which of the areas your marketing efforts are best focused.

- **How does the person become aware of the business or that particular product or service?**
- **Where are they likely to look for information?**
- **What things do they consider before they make a purchase?**
- **How do they evaluate your business after they have made a purchase?**
- **What factors are likely to help you to retain these customers?**

The Buying Process
There are a number of stages that people go through, either consciously or subconsciously, during the decision-making process of whether to buy.

- **Awareness**
- **Research**
- **Pre-purchase evaluation**
- **Post-purchase evaluation**

Raising awareness of your business
Right at the beginning of the buying process, your potential customer needs to become aware of your business. Here you need to think about how people find out about it. If you are already up and running, you could ask some of your customers directly and see whether any themes emerge. If you already know how people find out about you, you can focus your efforts on ensuring that you make the most of that very important first impression. Equally important, though, is to consider if there are any other ways in which you could raise awareness of your business. You could ask your customers where else they might have looked before they came across you.

If you are starting up a new business, this is an important question to consider. There needs to be a way, preferably several, for people to find out about you. You need to consider what your business is and what people normally do to find out about whom they can contact when they are looking for a particular product, service or expertise. Here it can be useful to have some idea of who your most successful competitors are, and research what they are doing that seems to work. Although you may not want to copy them exactly, it may help you to start thinking about what might work for you. Without trying, generally speaking, you will never know for sure whether or not a certain type of marketing works for you.

Case study: Tennis instructor

Let's take the example of a tennis instructor who offers both classes to groups of children and one-to-one tuition to children and adults. The instructor works alone on this business and it is a part-time activity, so not much time can be allocated to marketing.

The main target audience here is children and, since all children have to go to school, that can be an excellent opportunity to market to potential customers. One way in which this market could be reached is through any magazines or newsletters which are already distributed within the schools and local areas that you are targeting. You could produce your own material and then contact the schools individually to set up your distribution; however, it may be far more cost-effective and productive to use the distribution channels that are already in place, such as advertising in school newsletters or community magazines that are distributed through the schools.

Case study: Tennis school

Here we consider how the people running a tennis school, which consists of premises and five instructors, could think about raising awareness of their business. Since this is an established business, they are likely to be already getting word-of-mouth referrals. Other than promoting their business on the premises, no other marketing activities are performed. There is a fifty-fifty split between their adult and child customers.

Again, promoting directly to schools using existing distribution channels could be worthwhile. This would serve to raise their profile with the right audience, as well as getting exposure to the parents of the children and teachers who may also be interested. To reach the wider community, and because the tennis school is likely to have a larger budget to work with, they could consider placing advertisements in relevant newspapers and magazines. If feasible, it could also be beneficial to get editorials in the local press regarding newsworthy items, to generate free publicity. Competition results, outstanding achievement and talent in children as well as support for local good causes are all potentially newsworthy items.

Research and pre-purchase evaluation

Once people become aware of your business, they will then go through some form of evaluation before they make the decision to purchase from you. It can be helpful to find out what the factors were that they considered in checking whether your business was the right one to try. The location of your business, the age range you cater for, and the quality of your marketing materials could all be things that potential customers may take into account as part of their decision-making process.

Having an understanding of what the likely factors are can help you to ensure that your marketing materials, products and services make it absolutely clear whether you deliver against those criteria. Things they might consider before they purchase could include:

- **Your reputation**
- **Your branding and professionalism**
- **Your location**
- **The range of your other services and products**
- **Your qualifications and/or experience**
- **How you deal with beginners**
- **How you handle enquiries and friendliness of contact**
- **Trial lessons**
- **Information availability**
- **Comparison with your competitors**
- **Strength of word of mouth**
- **Ability to book without having to make contact**
- **Cost**
- **Ability to have some form of instant gratification**

Understanding what things people think about before they buy from you can help you to make sure that you are providing them with the information and the experience that they are looking for, so that you stand the best chance of successfully gaining them as your customers.

In order to aid this pre-purchase evaluation, potential customers may want to find out more about you. They may therefore go through a short period of research. You can simplify this process by making available information that will help them to conduct their pre-purchase evaluation of your business. This can take the form of:

- having all the relevant information available on a website
- having your contact details on all of your marketing materials so that you can be contacted with any questions
- ensuring that your marketing materials try to address the most common questions that potential customers ask during their pre-purchase evaluation phase

If you make it easier for potential customers to find out about your business and what you have to offer, it will be easier for them to take decisive action on whether or not to train with you. Not everybody will be willing to call you to discover more and so the more ways in which people can learn about you the better.

Post-purchase evaluation

Once a new customer has tried your product or service, they will go through some form of evaluation. Normally this can be quite informal and perhaps even subconscious. If they feel that they had a negative experience, they are unlikely to give you a second chance. Your business can be judged on how professionally it is conducted, how smooth the transaction and experience were, and even whether they feel that they liked it enough to try it again.

A good starting point for seeing how people evaluate your business is to ask any existing customers with whom you have a good relationship, and who are likely to give you some constructive and honest information. You can also think about how you yourself would evaluate the service or product if you were a customer buying from your business.

- How do they evaluate you after they have made a purchase?
- Did they feel that they received value for money?
- Did they enjoy the training?
- Did they like the people whom they met?
- Was the training fit for purpose for them?
- Was the training conducted in a professional manner?
- Were there many other people in the session, and did they enjoy being part of a group?
- Were there too many people in the session, and did they feel that they couldn't keep up?
- Were their needs and aspirations taken into account?
- Were the information and materials provided professional?
- How smooth was the induction into the business as a new customer?
- Were they made to feel welcome and valued?

Getting new customers is difficult and so it is a good idea to make the effort when people do come along to try out your business. Enduring relationships, positive word of mouth and your reputation can then start to yield new customers in the future and make your business a success.

You may want to consider putting in place either an informal or a formal evaluation process. An example of an informal process would be to simply speak to your customers after their first session and get any feedback directly. This is an excellent method for a sports or fitness professional, as it also helps to build the relationship with your new customer and make them feel valued and welcome. If you prefer a more formal approach, or the sheer number of students makes talking to everybody impossible, you may want to create a questionnaire that you can hand out to people at the end of a session to collect fresh feedback. The above list of questions should give you an idea of the kind of information that you may want to collect through your questionnaire. The more information you have about what you could do better, the easier it should be for you to make changes that will have a positive effect on your business as a whole.

Customer retention techniques

There will be certain factors that will make it easier for customers to return to you. For example, do you provide them with the relevant information on what their options are after their first transaction with you? Do you have a process in place for managing your customer contacts and also for getting in touch with them? If you provide coaching or instruction, is there a clear progression path or development plan that they would follow? Have you clearly defined the benefits of continuing their interaction with you? You could think about stressing:

- **Health benefits**
- **Certificate or grade progression**
- **Examinations**
- **Competitions**
- **Increase in ability through training**
- **Personal development plans**
- **Personal fitness targets**

Once your new customer has completed their induction into your business, are there clear options for how they could continue their custom with you? It is easy to take this kind of information for granted if you have been involved in your training for many years: but, for somebody new, a lot of the answers to these questions may not be obvious at all. It is your responsibility to make sure that all of your customers are aware of the benefits that they receive from training with you, and you need to do this through continual and reinforcing communication.

> ### Case study: Personal trainer
>
> If you are a personal trainer, you perhaps already create a development or training plan with your new client. Do you then have a process in place that, at appropriate intervals, re-evaluates the plan and targets as well as monitoring progress? Have you put in place a reward or recognition system that could help to encourage your clients? Is it clear what the benefits are from training with you, and what the timescales involved are in achieving those benefits?
>
> Some factors that are likely to help you to retain these customers are:
>
> - **Reliable service**
> - **Low cost**
> - **Friendly interaction**
> - **Variety of courses on offer throughout the year**

Have a go at exercise 4.1. It pulls together your understanding of the buying process that your customers might go through for each of your products and services. Don't worry if you have gaps at this stage. The idea is to start building up a picture of the buying process to help you to identify where you might need to focus your marketing efforts.

Exercise 4.1: List your services and products and answer the questions about the buying process. This will help you to find out where you might need to focus your marketing efforts.

LIST YOUR PRODUCTS AND SERVICES	HOW DO PEOPLE BECOME AWARE OF YOUR BUSINESS?	HOW DO PEOPLE RESEARCH YOUR BUSINESS?	WHAT FACTORS AFFECT THEIR PRE-PURCHASE EVALUATION?	WHAT FACTORS AFFECT THEIR POST-PURCHASE EVALUATION?	WHAT CUSTOMER RETENTION TECHNIQUES MAY BE EFFECTIVE?

CHAPTER 5
FOCUSING ON YOUR
STRENGTHS AND UNIQUENESS

Many sports and fitness professionals aren't able to market their business in a professional and consistent way and so there is a genuine chance that you can really benefit from any effort that you do make to run your business professionally and to approach it as any other business owner would. If you are starting up in business on your own, the chances are that you will also be responsible for actually doing all the marketing yourself. This may be something that you are comfortable with, or on the other hand the idea of doing marketing may worry you. It is not uncommon for sports and fitness professionals to have to do their own marketing, and the best way to deal with it is to use the skills that you have and then think about whether you can afford to get help. You can always consider using your network of family and friends to see if there is any way that they would be able to support you.

Do-it-yourself marketing or getting help?

You need to remember that you don't have to do everything yourself. You will need to balance the tasks that you take on personally and those which you decide to get help with or pay someone else to do for you. There are a number of things that are likely to affect your decision to do something yourself or to have it done by somebody else, including whether or not you have:

- **the right skills for the task, for example writing, design or computer skills**
- **the time to do the work yourself**
- **the money to pay someone else to do it for you**
- **somebody who could help you do something**
- **the time to find somebody who could help you do it**

Once you are a more established business, you may find it easier to pay for getting help with your marketing, especially if you feel that your profits from your business can justify the cost. If cost is an issue for your business, you can still achieve outstanding results through being innovative in the way that you market it. Pouring lots of money into marketing won't necessarily result in an increase in sales or completely remove having to put any effort into it. You will always need to direct your marketing efforts and be clear about what you want to achieve. Most people will find a natural balance of how much and what kind of marketing they are comfortable with and that is probably a good place to get started.

Relevant qualifications and experience

If there are things about you or your business that are likely to make you stand out or attract attention, it can be worthwhile highlighting these in your marketing. If, for example, you have completed some training or have some experience that can make your business distinctive, you should make sure that you display that information in your marketing. This unique information can help people to assess your professionalism and also to compare you with your competitors. Some potential customers may even be basing their choice of coach purely on qualifications or experience. For this reason, you need to make sure that you list any relevant qualifications and experience that you have. In fact, it can even be worth thinking about what additional qualifications and training you might want to gain that would make it easier to attract more business. Examples of relevant training could include:

- **Coaching qualifications that directly support what you coach, for example qualifications specific to the sport or type of fitness training**
- **Experience of receiving coaching, for example if you have trained with somebody famous or well respected, or internationally with masters in your field**
- **Competitions of note that you have won or taken part in**
- **Famous people whom you have coached**

You could mention how long you have been training and coaching and also whether you have any other qualifications or experience that are relevant but not directly related to what you are going to be coaching. For example:

- **First aid**
- **'How to coach' training**
- **Sports nutrition qualifications**
- **Developing athletes' training**
- **Long-term development of athletes' training**
- **Training in human anatomy and physiology**

Some sports and fitness training may have coaching standards and qualifications that you need to adhere to and so it would be worth finding out about those too, as potential customers are likely to ask about them. In exercise 5.1, list the relevant qualifications and experience that you already have and also what additional training you think would attract more customers to your coaching business.

Exercise 5.1: List your current relevant qualifications and experience and then list any training that you think would help your business in the future.

CURRENT RELEVANT QUALIFICATIONS AND EXPERIENCE

POTENTIAL FUTURE TRAINING IDEAS

Your unique combination of experience and qualifications may be what attracts some customers to your business, so make sure that you include that information in your marketing where appropriate. You need to ensure that both new and current customers are aware of your professional development, as it helps to remind them why they want to keep doing business with you. Knowing that you are continually looking for ways to increase the value that you deliver to your customers should help to strengthen your business.

A celebrity in your field

If you have competed at a national or an international level in your field, you may be well known to those who are interested in that sport. If you are a celebrity in your field and you have decided to set up your own sports or fitness school, you need to remember that, if you are marketing to the general public, not everyone will be aware of who you are. In fact, it is often the case that your clients may just be there purely for what you are teaching rather than your celebrity status.

If you have reached some sort of celebrity status in your field, it can be worthwhile making that clear in your marketing. You may find that some new clients are drawn to your business simply because they are interested in meeting you. Examples of things that could lead to people's according you such status include having:

- **appeared on TV or in a movie**
- **won national or international competitions**
- **competed in the Olympic Games or the Commonwealth Games**
- **written a book**
- **written for trade magazines**
- **developed a popular website on your area of expertise**
- **appeared regularly in newspapers or magazines**

Even indirect fame could boost your business profile – but only if you let people know about what you have done. This won't necessarily influence every single client, but it can certainly add to your reputation and improve your customer retention rates. Creating this kind of a unique offering can really help you to stand out from your competitors, and it won't be something that they can easily copy.

Review your other skills and those of your network

It can be worthwhile writing down what skills you think you have that you could use to help with your marketing. These could include:

- **Design**
- **Creating artwork**
- **Photography**
- **Word processing to create leaflets and other content such as articles**
- **Writing**
- **Researching on the Internet**
- **Developing web pages**
- **Programming databases, including online databases**
- **Using off-the-shelf software**
- **Sales**
- **Communicating on the phone and by email**
- **Presenting information**
- **Customer service**
- **Organisation**

From the list above, you can see that there is a whole range of skills that you can bring to bear if you are planning to do your own marketing. If you do not have certain skills, there may be people within your network of family and friends whom you might be able to ask for help. Think about whether they have any skills that would be useful to you and list them in exercise 5.2.

Exercise 5.2: List other skills that you or your network have which can help you in your marketing efforts.

AVAILABILITY	HOW COULD THAT HELP YOU?	WHO HAS THEM?	SKILLS

Understanding what skills you have can help you to focus on marketing activities that are likely to play to your strengths. This is especially important if you are planning to do it all alone, as do many sports and fitness professionals to start with. If you feel that you have gaps in your available skill set, you may find that, after you have decided on which marketing techniques are most suitable for your business, you will need to look into hiring some support.

CHAPTER 6
PLANNING TO MAKE
MARKETING EASIER

From the previous chapters, you should have a good idea about why marketing is important for sports and fitness professionals and how it may be able to help you in your coaching business endeavours. We have also looked at how you could develop your business offering and considered essential areas such as identifying your target market and understanding how they might make their decision to purchase from you. Being clear about your strengths and weaknesses will also help you to understand how best you can approach marketing activity and how that could work around the skills which you already have. This chapter looks at consolidating your ideas of what your coaching activities really are by creating a programme, which will then enable you to design your marketing programme. Knowing what coaching you are offering in the next year will help you to focus on making sure that you market those services well and in good time ahead of, say, any courses or classes starting. Creating your marketing plan is covered in part III of this book.

The vision for your business

Having a vision of what you would want your business to look like in the future can help you to design the kind of coaching programme and marketing you should be offering today. If you have a vision of running pay-as-you-go classes that are well attended, you will need to start working on building up a customer base and a mechanism for attracting new customers to those classes. If you have a vision of running an exclusive fitness business, you will need to design your coaching programme, pricing and marketing to reflect that. Once you have your vision in place, you can use this as a way of always double checking any ideas. If they fit in with your business vision and support your getting there, then at least you know that your efforts are helping you to get closer to achieving your goal.

Case study: Personal trainer

A personal trainer thinks about what her business would look like in the future if it was successful, and has a vision of:

- **Creating a workout regime of her own that she would promote**
- **Being selective about the clients with whom she personally worked**
- **Having a team of trainers working for her to whom she could direct additional work**

- Having her own fitness centre from which to operate
- Establishing franchises to extend the format of her business across the country
- Being able to earn a living through working part-time so that she would have time to spend with her family
- Having motivation to stay fit over the longer term

In the case study of a personal trainer, you can see a very personal vision of her future business. Each of the goals listed can be matched directly to the kinds of marketing activity that could help the personal trainer to achieve them. Let's take each of the goals in turn and see what the personal trainer could do to help her progress towards meeting them.

1. Creating a workout regime of her own that she would promote

You need to create an identity for your unique training programme and perhaps even a brand for it. You can work on building the reputation of your programme through magazine articles and perhaps books and videos.

2. & 3. Being selective about the clients with whom she personally worked and having a team of trainers working for her to whom she could direct additional work

If you want to be selective about the clients whom you work with, you can set your pricing and brand identity so that they appeal to the right kind of people. Having the ability to take on staff or to pass on other work, while also taking a cut, will make it easier for you to be selective about the work that you do. For this reason, you should always keep a lookout for ways in which you could find and encourage people to work for you or with you.

4. Having her own fitness centre from which to operate

If you aspire to have your own fitness centre, you will need to think about how you will fund it, where it should be located and how you will ensure that your business model works out so that you can afford it. If you are not in a position to have your own centre yet, you may want to focus your marketing efforts in the area that you wish to eventually be, so that you build up clients in that region who can immediately join your centre as soon as it opens.

5. Establishing franchises to extend the format of her business across the country

If you hope to be able to sell franchises of your business, then branding, building a reputation and developing appropriate materials such as intellectual assets will all be important. If you have this in mind, you can start thinking about making sure that the marketing materials that you create today can also be reused in some form in the future.

6. Being able to earn a living through working part-time so that she would have time to spend with her family

If you want to be able to earn a living through your business and still have time left over to spend with your family, you need to think about how you will attract staff to your business. Creating a business that is professional and desirable to be associated with can help to attract staff to you. You would also need to think about how you will structure your coaching programme and marketing materials if you are planning to use other instructors as well.

7. Having motivation to stay fit over the longer term

If you are in the personal training business as a way of ensuring that you look after yourself over the long term as well, you want to ensure that you design your products and services in a way that will enable you to still get what you want out of your business. One of the most common mistakes that trainers make is that they start a business and then, even if they are successful, they begin to get bored from doing the same old thing over and over again. However, it is this very reliability and consistency of service that your customers will be looking for. So, if you plan to pick and choose the elements of the coaching that you take on yourself, you will need to ensure that you have a way to meet other customer demands or you will risk losing their business.

Your vision

The vision of your business can help you to direct your marketing efforts, and to home in on the right customers and locations. Make a note of any ideas that you have for your business vision in exercise 6.1.

Exercise 6.1: List the goals that you have that help to make up your business vision.

1.
2.
3.
4.

5.
6.
7.
8.
9.
10.

Customer development planning

When you are thinking about what your coaching programme should look like, you might want to also consider how your customers can progress with your classes. Through your training they should be gaining skills and getting better. If this is the case, it can be worthwhile to have a clear pathway that you have set up for people to follow as they improve. This might be through offering different classes for different skill or experience levels, or you might just keep different intakes separate.

Case study: Progression of coaching services for a beginner student

A set process for the way a beginner student can progress through the variety of classes that are offered may be as follows:

- Attend an introductory session
- Join a regular class
- Occasionally attend a premium class
- Occasionally look for personal training
- Move on to intermediate and advanced level classes as appropriate

Have a go at exercise 6.2 and see if you can think of ways in which you could offer coaching that would cater for a student's development.

Exercise 6.2: Note your ideas for the ways in which you could offer coaching to make it match a student's development.

1.
2.
3.
4.
5.
6.

Professional development planning

As well as planning the coaching programme for your business, you may also want to think about what you would like to offer in the future, or at least what additions you could make to your business that could result in increased revenue. Once you know what you would like your business to achieve in the next few years, you can focus on how you need to develop in order to meet those challenges. You may find that it is not always a sports- or fitness-related qualification or experience that is needed. In many cases, you may identify that you have a requirement in some other business area, where an improvement would make it easier for you to run your business. For example:

- **You find business administration and managing all the paperwork difficult.**
- **You have trouble doing your own bookkeeping and so perhaps evening classes would help you to develop some basic skills.**
- **You need to work on your interaction with customers and your confidence in being able to communicate with them.**

In general, there is no point in spending time on a qualification or training for your business unless you can clearly see what benefit it will have. You will also need to consider whether it makes more sense for you to just outsource some parts of the business to help you stay focused on delivering the sports and fitness side. However, you won't be able to disassociate yourself from all business considerations, so it can be helpful to start obtaining some supporting business training. Some examples of training that might be helpful include:

- **How to set up a business**
- **Business administration**
- **Record keeping**
- **Book-keeping**
- **Dealing with customers**
- **Taking on staff and managing people**

That is not to say that you should not also consider how you can improve your own sports or fitness offering through gaining more qualifications and training. As well as giving you more confidence and additional stamps of approval that you can show to potential customers, it will also act as a way of keeping you motivated and excited about what you are doing. This is particularly the case with personal trainers or sports coaches who find that they spend most of their time teaching the same things over and over again. It can be helpful to expand your own knowledge and experience base to keep you fresh and energised about your business.

You may have only one coaching style, which may not work with all of your students. Going on 'how to coach' training may give you an insight into different ways in which you can coach. This will make coaching more exciting for you, giving you options on how to explain things when people get stuck, and it will also mean that your students benefit from a varied style.

You may even want to consider training that will directly help you to improve your marketing, for example:

- **Writing for marketing**
- **Photography**
- **Computer skills**
- **Specific software skills, such as word processing and using spread-sheets**

Have a go at exercise 6.3 and see if you can think of ways in which you could work on your own professional development.

Exercise 6.3: Note your ideas for the ways in which you could work on your own professional development in support of your business.

1.	
2.	
3.	
4.	
5.	

Create a programme

Spending specific and dedicated time on managing the planning process will enable you to think about your business as a whole without being distracted by day-to-day operational activities. This will mean that you should be able to focus on identifying the activities that will make a long-term difference while de-prioritising those that won't have a lasting effect. When you are busy firefighting and dealing with customers, it can be difficult to keep focus on the things that really matter. You have to be able to step back and distinguish between activities that will add real value to your business and those that just keep you busy without moving your business forwards.

Identify your milestones

When you start thinking about pulling together a plan of activities for your business, if you have never done it before it can feel quite daunting. A good way to start is using mind maps.

Using mind maps

Mind maps are simply a structured way of brainstorming ideas. In this way, you can start collecting all of your thoughts in one place. It doesn't matter about getting all the details exactly right yet. You just want to focus on trying to get all the relevant themes identified. Follow the steps below to create your mind map:

1 On the centre of the page write down the name of your coaching business.
2 Write down all the main activities, events or milestones that you can think of which you will be doing for your business in the next year. Have them coming off your centre circle, joined to it by lines.
3 If you wish, create additional branches to represent hierarchies of activities.

You can then take a look at your mind map and see whether there is a number of distinct categories that you have identified. You may be able to group some together and you may need to expand on others. Take a look at the mind map example in figure 1 (*see* opposite): this may help you to get started in creating one of your own.

Using brainstorming

If mind maps don't work for you, you could simply try the following:

1 Make a list of your expected activities, events and milestones for the next year.
2 Take a look at this list and see whether you can group the items into broad categories.
3 Reorder the items and check if you think you have missed anything out. Look at both the categories and the items within the categories to see if you can identify anything else.

Categorising your ideas

If you are having trouble thinking of categories, have a look at some of those listed below and consider if they can help you to come up with a suitable way to approach your plan.

- Communications
- Internal processes development
- Coaching programme
- Professional development programme
- Long-term business development and growth

Figure 1: Mind map example

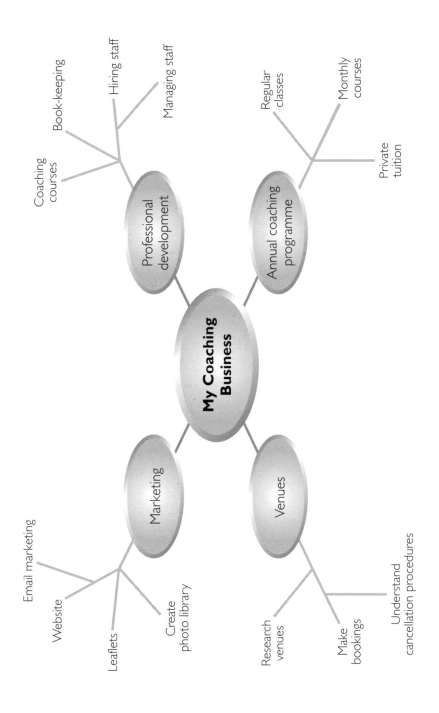

You may be able to categorise your milestones by theme, for example communication both internally to staff and externally to customers as appropriate, or you may have a bunch of internal processes that you would like to get into place in the coming year, such as forms for new members to complete and some way of giving your customers further information about your products and services. You may have a good idea of what kind of programme you would like to offer your customers in the coming year. You want to have all of these ideas and milestones captured in your plan. And, of particular relevance to this book, you ought to have a section on marketing.

High-, Medium- and Low-Priority Milestones

In addition to categorising your milestones by activity type, you may also want to differentiate between the milestones on the basis of priority. For example, some milestones may be far more important than others and it may be essential that those are done, whereas others may well be nice to have but won't damage your business if they are delayed by a year. You should think about adding the additional categorisation of high, medium and low priority to your milestones.

Develop your one-year programme

Now put your milestones onto the template for a one-year programme in exercise 6.4. This will give you a simple one-page plan that you can quickly reference and use to keep you on track throughout the year.

Exercise 6.4: List your separate milestone categories in the first column of the one-year programme. Then place a diamond to mark the position and date of your milestone and write a short description next to it.

CATEGORY	JAN	FEB	MAR	APR	MAY	JUN	JUL	AUG	SEP	OCT	NOV	DEC

> **Case study: Sample one-year programme for a personal trainer**
> Take the example of a personal trainer just starting out in business on his own. His sample programme shows the categories, and milestones within those categories, that he has identified.

Table 6.1: Sample one-year programme for a personal trainer

CATEGORY	Milestone	JAN	FEB	MAR	APR	MAY	JUN	JUL	AUG	SEP	OCT	NOV	DEC
PROGRAMME	BEGINNERS' TRIAL CLASSES	◆											
	COURSES				◆			◆			◆		
MARKETING	Posters and leaflets at the venue	◆											
	Advert or editorial in local newspaper	◆											
	Promote beginners' trial classes on the website	◆											
	Promote the courses	◆											
	Prepare the following year's marketing plan									◆			
	Promote the following year's classes and courses									◆			
INTERNAL PROCESSES	Create a process for managing customer information		◆										
	Prepare an information leaflet to give to new clients			◆									
	Create a filing system for managing the paperwork				◆								
PERSONAL DEVELOPMENT	Prepare the following year's programme and update five-year programme									◆			
	Prepare the following year's marketing plan and update five-year programme									◆			
	Research training and development options						◆						
	Book the selected options									◆			
	Complete qualifications												◆

As you can see from the one-year programme in the case study, in this way you can start putting together a really good idea of what you want to achieve. Every time that you have a new idea, you can look at your plan and see how best you can fit it in and whether it makes sense given all the other activities that you are doing. Then each year, when you come to do a new plan, you can use the one that you have done before as a starting point. If you complete activities, you can take them off and if you haven't, you can move them onto the next year's plan. During the year, you can simply update the plan as you go along.

The kinds of thing that you can put into the marketing section of your plan are the topic of part II of this book. Part III then looks at how you can pull together the marketing section of your plan and manage it.

Develop your five-year business programme

You may feel that you have an idea of what you would like the next five years to look like for your business. If you do, it is a good idea to get that written down straight away. It doesn't matter that your ideas may change over time. Having a plan means that you have somewhere to park your ideas and to develop them as your business grows. The kinds of thing that you may want to consider adding to your five-year plan could include:

- **Offering quarterly courses**
- **Coming up with a way to get new students through trial lessons**
- **Trying to find work in schools**
- **Offering private tuition**
- **Trying to find work through local businesses**
- **Hiring staff**

You could photocopy the template in exercise 6.5 and fill it in by hand. This way you have a simple five-year plan that you can add to at any time. You can use this to help you to develop your business vision and to think about how you may want to grow your business.

Exercise 6.5: List your separate milestone categories in the first column of the five-year programme. Then place a diamond to mark the position of your milestone and write a short description next to it.

CATEGORY	YEAR 1	YEAR 2	YEAR 3	YEAR 4	YEAR 5

CHAPTER 7
MAKING MARKETING A CORE BUSINESS ACTIVITY

Marketing is not a one-off activity. Some might think that you can just assign a week to marketing activities and then not have to do any marketing-related work throughout the year. Wouldn't it be great to then focus all of your efforts on actually coaching the clients who come to you? If this is the case, the marketing plan that you are following may well be too onerous for you. Marketing is something that you should be doing on an ongoing basis. It is better for you to think about what you put in your marketing plan that personally works for you. If you find it difficult to fit it in, or if it makes you uncomfortable, you probably won't be getting the best out of that activity anyway. It is much better to keep it simple and practical, so that you can follow your marketing plan without having to think about it too much. Ideally, you want marketing to become second nature to you. The more marketing you do, the more you build the brand, awareness and reputation of your business. Steady, consistent and ongoing effort is normally what is required. If you can make marketing a regular and undividable part of your business efforts, you may find that it will seem less onerous and work much better in the long run.

Marketing goals

The previous chapter looked at putting together some plans for your business. Once you are clear on where you are today and where you want to be in the future, you can start thinking in more detail about how you can achieve that through your marketing. You may want to start developing better-defined marketing goals, such as increasing awareness of your sport or business. Or perhaps you are looking to increase the number of:

- **enquiries**
- **members**
- **new customers**
- **returning customers**
- **customers from a particular region**
- **customers during a particular season**

You always need to keep your marketing goals in mind when you are deciding what marketing techniques to use and how you might best apply them.

Marketing budget

There are many ways in which you can think about your marketing budget. Should you even have one at all? Some people prefer to work with budgets and have an understanding of how much they can afford to spend on what. However, wouldn't it be wonderful if you could get all of your marketing done very cheaply or even for free? If you are starting out in business for yourself, the last thing you want to do is to lose your own money on marketing activities that don't result in any work for you. Surely you should aim to spend the least that you can while getting the best value possible. That doesn't mean that you shouldn't do anything at all, or that you should only choose things that are cheap to do.

There are many ways in which you can be creative about how you use your money on marketing, and you can also be creative at finding ways to get excellent marketing for your business at very little or no cost. Often, these creative ways may take more time than money. However, if you are new to starting up in business, you may feel that you have more time than money to dedicate to things. That is fine too. Whatever the mix of time and money you have available to you, you should be able to find ways in which you can market your business. The main thing to remember is that you are aiming to get a result in terms of increased sales, or customers, or exposure. You just need to be focused on your marketing objectives and make sure that you direct your efforts to meeting them effectively.

Attitude to marketing

Marketing certainly isn't something that everybody is comfortable with. You may hate the idea of having to go and talk to people or to research ways in which you could market your business. If this is you, then you could make a start by having a go at exercise 7.1, which asks you to list the things that make you worried about marketing and those, if any, that excite you about it.

Exercise 7.1: List the things about marketing that excite you and worry you.

EXCITE
1.
2.

3.
4.
5.
6.

WORRY

1.
2.
3.
4.
5.
6.

Maybe the things that excite you about marketing include:

- **Meeting new people**
- **Learning a new skill**
- **Finding new ways in which to reach potential customers**
- **Seeing the success of your marketing efforts**

Perhaps some of the things that worry you about marketing are:

- **Having to call people to find out about things such as newspaper listings**
- **Returning calls for customer enquiries**
- **Seeing your business promoted everywhere**

- Speaking on the phone
- Doing paperwork and the amount of work involved
- Looking silly
- People finding out about what you are doing
- Not looking professional

All of these reasons are the things that real people have worried about. Listing your likes and dislikes in exercise 7.1 should help you to identify how you feel about marketing. Once you have pinned that down, you can then think clearly about which marketing activities you are going to feel most comfortable trying. If you don't match the two, you might find that you have all the right ideas but cannot motivate yourself to follow them through. It is much better to start with small and achievable marketing efforts and then to build them up as your experience and confidence grow. Remember that you need to start somewhere, and hopefully as you start to see the fruits of your labour you will also begin to enjoy the marketing process far more.

Make your marketing achievable

If you are just getting started in marketing for the first time, remember to make sure that the marketing tasks that you set yourself are achievable for you. You may later decide that they weren't quite right or that they would have been more effective if you had done them in some different way. The fact is that, unless you try, you may never actually find out what works for you and your business.

Part II of this book looks at a range of different marketing techniques. The idea isn't to overwhelm you with the number of things you should be doing, but rather to present to you a host of activities that you could try either straight away or at some point in the future once your business is more established. At any one time, it is best to have a number of different marketing activities working for you. Keeping approximately between three and ten types of activity going is a great start. Some will work and others won't. Some will be more successful than others, even though they may have required little effort. So, once you get started, you can keep the activities that work and then perhaps each year try a couple of new ones. As you build up your experience, you may find that it gets easier and that you start gaining enough of a reputation and awareness of your business that free promotional opportunities start to come your way. When they do come your way, you want to make sure that you are ready to make the most of them. If you keep working at your marketing, it should get easier and your business should grow.

Keep Marketing!

Stopping marketing can mark the first stage of a decline in your business, as in effect you stop priming your business pipeline with new customers. Effective marketing should always keep new customers coming to you.

PART II
TECHNIQUES

CHAPTER 8
PICK AND MIX YOUR MARKETING TECHNIQUES

In this part of the book, you will take what you have learned in part I to help you to pick the right mix of marketing activities. Try to bear in mind the exercises that you completed in part I and what you learned about your business and your skill set. If it has been some time since you did that, just take a quick look again at those exercises now to refresh your memory about what you are trying to achieve with your marketing and exactly what services you are trying to promote using each of the marketing techniques. To summarise, in part I of this book we looked at the following topics:

- **The importance of marketing for sports and fitness professionals**
- **Developing your business offering**
- **Identifying your customers**
- **Understanding how your customers make purchases**
- **Focusing on your strengths and uniqueness**
- **Planning to make marketing easier**
- **Making marketing a core business activity**

Introduction to part II

The remaining chapters of this part of the book present a range of different types of marketing activity that you could try. As you work through these chapters, you should bear in mind your marketing objectives and your skills as you start to think about and select the activities that you might try first. Don't worry – this isn't a list that can't be changed later. Marketing is an ongoing and iterative process and so you can always try other techniques later on.

Offline marketing techniques

Chapters 9 to 11 cover entry-level, intermediate and advanced traditional marketing techniques. By traditional we basically mean that these are offline ways of promoting your business that have traditionally been used by sports and fitness professionals. You can select any combination of techniques from these chapters that you are comfortable with.

Chapter 9: Entry-level traditional marketing techniques

This chapter looks at some basic marketing techniques that should be relatively easy in terms of getting started with. Often used by sports and fitness professionals, these include:

- Using photography skills
- Using computer skills
- Using design skills
- Getting referrals from family and friends
- Getting listed in local directories
- Advertising
- Offering coupons and discounts
- Distributing leaflets
- Putting up posters
- Offering product samples and taster lessons
- Building your brand

Any design work or writing requirements in the list above are kept to a minimum by choosing techniques that enable you to get something quickly drawn up, either by yourself or with straightforward help from someone else.

Chapter 10: Intermediate traditional marketing techniques

The marketing techniques covered in this chapter are ones that may require a bit more effort than those in chapter 9, particularly if you are completely new to marketing. They may also be easier once you are a little more established and have a solid client base. These are:

- Using writing skills
- Using direct mail
- Creating brochures
- Generating free publicity
- Getting word-of-mouth referrals
- Using customer testimonials
- Running demonstrations

Chapter 11: Advanced traditional marketing techniques

There are a number of more advanced marketing techniques that are great for sports and fitness professionals. We are lucky in that the sports and fitness business is a very visual one and this means that there are plenty of ways in which you could try to harness that creatively in order to promote your business. Given that coaching has much in common with presenting and teaching, you can think about what other approaches are available in order for you to harness existing skills in different ways. The techniques covered in chapter 11 are listed below.

- Using creativity
- Writing books

- Creating DVDs
- Developing your own merchandise

Online marketing techniques

Chapter 12 is the final chapter in part II of this book and looks specifically at online ways of promoting your business.

Chapter 12: Electronic marketing techniques

If you have some computer skills, you will of course be able to harness them in the implementation of some of the techniques covered in chapters 9 to 11; however, this chapter looks at using more advanced computer skills, such as using email for marketing, and using spreadsheets and specialised software to help you run your business while at the same time helping you to promote it. The topics covered in this chapter are:

- Using email and mailing lists
- Developing a website
- Using electronic newsletters and magazines
- Using customer management systems
- Using membership management systems

Techniques appropriate for you

As you work through part II of this book, think about which marketing techniques would be appropriate for which of your coaching services and products. Write down your ideas in exercise 8.1.

Exercise 8.1: List all of your coaching services and products in the space below. As you work your way through part II of this book, you can note down any ideas that you have about which marketing techniques would be appropriate for promoting which item.

1.	
2.	
3.	
4.	
5.	
6.	
7.	
8.	
9.	

You may find that your understanding of some of the topics covered in part I of this book improves as you start thinking about how to promote your business. For example, you might have an idea either for a new kind of product that you could try selling or for how you could offer a slightly different type of class. You should make sure that you capture all of your ideas – even if it means going back to part I of this book to make some notes. If you decide that you don't want to try out that idea immediately, at least you have it written down somewhere where you can find it later if you decide you need it.

What's in part III?

Part III of this book looks at taking the information that you have put together in the exercises of parts I and II to develop your very own tailor-made marketing plan. At this stage, you can consider whether you want to make any changes to the marketing techniques that you have chosen or the number that you think you are realistically able to try. Part III also looks at a number of other aspects of marketing that you can incorporate as part of your ongoing marketing process. The topics covered in part III are:

- **Preparing your tailor-made marketing plan**
- **Measuring effectiveness**
- **Managing customer service**
- **The ongoing marketing process**

Get customers now

Some marketing activities will have the potential to generate quick results for you and others may take time to do so. For example, letting your family and friends know that you are starting up as a personal trainer and asking them if they can each recommend three people they know, whom you could contact to offer your services, could be a good way to get customers quickly to help you get started. However, your family and friends may not have an endless supply of people whom they can ask, and so you will need to have other marketing activities that can bring other people to you in the future.

Conversely, if you are planning to secure customers through a website, that may not yield results for you immediately. It will take time to design and develop the website, for customers to find it using search engines and for you to go to listings and other websites to get them to add links and referrals to your business. This can be quite worthwhile, but a very lengthy process nonetheless.

So, when you are thinking about which marketing techniques to try, remember that some may work faster than others, and at all times bear in mind what you are trying to achieve through your marketing to ensure that you have a sensible mix of marketing techniques with which to get started.

Complying with data protection legislation

Whenever you are considering processing personal information on people in any way, you should make sure that you are complying with all relevant data protection legislation. Individuals also have a right to find out what personal information is held on computer and most paper records. In general terms, you must ensure that the information is:

- **accurate and up to date**
- **adequate, relevant and not excessive**
- **fairly and lawfully processed**
- **not kept for longer than is necessary**
- **not transferred to other countries without adequate protection**
- **processed for limited purposes**
- **processed in line with people's rights**
- **secure**

You should ensure that you keep up to date with all data protection legislation and comply with such legislation throughout all of your marketing efforts.

Meeting your marketing objectives

A good way to keep yourself focused on which marketing techniques you should choose is to fill in exercise 8.2 as you work through the chapters of this part of the book. Then you can review your basket of marketing techniques to ensure that you have chosen in a way that sufficiently captures what you are hoping to achieve with your marketing. The point of this exercise is to help you to focus on picking activities that will directly meet your marketing objectives. If you pick activities that don't meet one of your marketing objectives, you need to consider whether you have missed out an important marketing objective or whether you should discard those activities completely for the time being.

Exercise 8.2: List your marketing objectives in the first column and then fill in the marketing techniques alongside each of your objectives as you select them. Identify which of your services you can promote using that technique and also which of your skills you will need to use.

MY SKILLS	SERVICES	TECHNIQUE	MARKETING OBJECTIVE

Pick and mix your marketing techniques

Now you are ready to have a look at a number of different marketing techniques that you could try. Don't forget your marketing objectives and what you have learned about your business as you pick which marketing techniques you'd like to try!

CHAPTER 9
ENTRY-LEVEL TRADITIONAL
MARKETING TECHNIQUES

There are a number of fairly quick and easy traditional marketing techniques that you could try. If you are completely new to marketing, these can be some simple ways that you can get started on. Once you feel comfortable with some of these, you could see whether you are confident enough to try some activities from the later chapters. Alternatively, you may feel that a selection from each of the chapters may suit you the best.

Using your photography skills

Pictures can really help to support all of your marketing efforts and cut down on design work. If you create a portfolio of pictures that you can use as you wish in whatever form of marketing, it can make it easier and faster for you to produce all kinds of eye-catching marketing material. You can use photos in free publicity opportunities or add them to:

- **leaflets, posters and brochures**
- **advertisements**
- **your website**

Photos can be useful to show the range of students whom you take on. Also, as a sports or fitness professional, you probably have excellent opportunities for capturing interesting still and action shots of:

- **training exercises**
- **sports and fitness equipment**
- **competitions and winners**

Digital photography can provide you with a cheap way to create and manage your photographs. You could even look into photo-editing software, which can help you to make better use of your photo library, for example by adding effects and cutting out pictures so that you can use them as background images.

Table 9.1: Using your photography skills

Description	Making use of the photography skills that you already have and applying them to all of your marketing efforts.

Why it works for sports and fitness businesses	Sports or fitness training is an excellent source of material for capturing interesting photographs.
Cost	Negligible if you already have your own digital camera and a computer.
Advantages	Can be used in all kinds of marketing to attract customers.
Disadvantages	Dependent on how comfortable you are with photography and using photo-editing software.

Using your computer skills

If you are proficient at using word processors, presentation software or even graphics packages, being able to quickly create your own marketing materials could save you a lot of time and money. You could use these resources as follows:

- **Word processors: for creating leaflets, brochures and articles**
- **Presentation software: for creating posters and even leaflets**
- **Graphics packages: for modifying digital photos or for creating graphics, logos and posters**
- **Spreadsheets: for managing customer information**

If you have computer skills, these will be very useful to you should you decide to do a lot of your own marketing. It is of course possible to pay for having design work done for you and so you could reduce your own computer work if you wanted to.

Table 9.2: Using your computer skills

Description	Making use of the computer skills that you already have and applying them to all of your marketing efforts.
Why it works for sports and fitness businesses	A lot of sports and fitness professionals who start off by creating and managing their own marketing materials can utilise computer skills to make these tasks easier.

Cost	Negligible if you already have a computer. You can even get a lot of good software for free if you have Internet access, so this expense can be avoided too.
Advantages	Can enable you to quickly create marketing materials as well as making it easier for you to update them in the future.
Disadvantages	If you are not comfortable using a computer, you may find this quite difficult.

Using your design skills

Regardless of whether you are good at using computers, if you do your own marketing, or even if you have somebody else do it for you, you can make great use of any design skills that you have. Remember that nobody knows your business better than you do, so you should have the best idea of what may or may not work for your business. Designing is all about being able to come up with design ideas and then implementing them. But you have to come up with the idea first. If you have a sense of what looks good together and how things can be visually combined to form a strong and coherent message, you have some valuable skills that your business could make use of by bringing together words and pictures in a unique way.

Table 9.3: Using your design skills

Description	Making use of your creativity and the design skills that you already have and applying them to all of your marketing efforts.
Why it works for sports and fitness businesses	Good design can help to give your coaching business a strong identity and make it stand out from the competition.
Cost	Negligible except for your time.
Advantages	Can enable you to quickly create marketing materials as well as making it easier for you to update them in the future.
Disadvantages	Designing your own materials can be time consuming and this may not be the best use of your time.

Getting referrals from family and friends

Many sports and fitness businesses that are just starting out get their first customers in this way. Don't underestimate how important it can be to boost your morale to have some customers right from when you start your new business. This can be an easy way to help you get up and running. Simply let your family and friends know that you have started up a coaching business and what kinds of student you are looking for. Ask them if they can specifically recommend two or three people to your business. You will need to be able to explain your business or service offering in a simple way that they will be able to remember. Exercise 1.3 in chapter 1, on describing your business in no more than three sentences, should be of help here. It is important to take note of the relevant data protection legislation that applies to the way in which you decide to collect and use any information.

The great thing about asking your family and friends for referrals is that there is virtually no marketing expense associated with it. If you happen to have leaflets or a business card to hand out to them to give to potential customers, that may help them to pass on your information. Another advantage of this technique is that it will cost little in terms of your time as well.

An advantage of getting referrals is that it has the potential to secure customers very quickly. And if you are starting up a new business, this can help to get you started on the right track, build your confidence and try out your training and coaching methods. The main downside to this method is that your family and friends may run out of people whom they can refer to you, particularly if they are in an environment where they aren't meeting new people all the time.

Table 9.4: Getting referrals from family and friends

Description	Asking your family and friends to recommend your coaching business to people whom they know or to send you potential clients' contact details for you to follow up.
Why it works for sports and fitness businesses	They may know people who are keen to try out new sports or activities – either adults, or families where there are children of the appropriate age. You could be giving them the opportunity to try something out in a comfortable environment.
Cost	None.

Advantages	This can be an easy and inexpensive way to help you get customers when you have just started up.
Disadvantages	Your family and friends may quickly run out of people whom they can recommend, and you will probably have to find other ways to gain new customers.

Getting listed in directories

These are simple line listings in, for example, the Yellow Pages, the business pages and other relevant directories, including online directories. You should aim to get details such as your business name, address, telephone numbers, email and website information included. For most customers, the location of the training may be really important. They will want to train close to their home, workplace or other place that they visit regularly. For this reason, some people are likely to search in local business directories to find out what sports and fitness services are on offer in their local area. If you aren't listed there, you could miss out on potential customers.

Directories tend to have a good shelf life in homes and so your information could be available to potential customers for a long time after you initially place your listing. The great thing about directories is that, once you have placed your listing, there is no distribution for you to worry about – that will all be done for you. Many directories offer free listings, which are very basic. You should certainly try to get listed for free and then, if you find that this method of getting customers works for you, you might consider actually paying for advertisements in the same directories. The paid-for advertisements will generally allow you to give more information and to make your content more attractive so that it is more likely to catch somebody's eye.

Table 9.5: Getting listed in directories

Description	Simple line listings of your business in local business and sports and fitness directories, giving information such as your business name and contact details.
Why it works for sports and fitness businesses	If people are looking to train locally, they are likely to look in local business directories to find out what sports and fitness services are available in the area.
Cost	Many directories offer the opportunity of having simple, text-based listings for free.

Advantages	They are low cost or even free and can potentially reach a large number of people.
Disadvantages	You may need to keep going back to the directory to update your information each year.

Advertising

Advertising in the local media can be one of the most expensive ways of marketing when you are starting up in business. You will need to consider the areas that the newspaper is distributed in and whether the services that you are offering are likely to appeal to the people. You also need to assess if a single advert alone will be noticed enough to generate any business for you. Or should you be considering some kind of regular advertising feature?

Table 9.6: Advertising

Description	Paying for your presence in the local media.
Why it works for sports and fitness businesses	Many sports and fitness professionals tend to work in their local area. If this is the case, advertising in the local press could be advantageous.
Cost	Can work out quite expensive. However, prices can normally be negotiated down quite heavily if you are willing to have a go.
Advantages	You can reach a large number of people very quickly. If you are working on your own, having somebody else take care of distribution can be a huge weight off your mind.
Disadvantages	Can be costly. Also, don't forget that your advert may be thrown out unread with the paper and so the actual number of people who see it will be smaller than the distribution numbers quoted by the paper.

Offering coupons and discounts

Many sports and fitness professionals try offering discounted first lessons, or even the first or first few lessons free. You'll need to think about how you can offer discounts, while ensuring that the addition of new people does not affect the quality of the service that your other students receive. Make sure that you are clear about the costs to you of offering such discounts and whether they are sustainable.

You will have to think carefully about what kinds of promotion you could offer. Some possibilities are:

- **First training session free**
- **First five training sessions free**
- **Reduced rate for new customers**
- **Reduced rate for the first year for new customers**

Table 9.7: Offering coupons and discounts

Description	You can offer free or reduced price training in order to try to attract people to your business.
Why it works for sports and fitness businesses	This is a good way to let people have a go at your training without their feeling that they are spending money on something which they may not enjoy.
Cost	You will obviously take a hit on lost revenue as well as potentially having to pay for a training venue out of your own pocket. However, you may be able to cleverly design your promotion so that there is no additional cost to you.
Advantages	Creates a low-risk environment for people to come and try your business out. If you distribute coupons, for example, in a newspaper, you can track the success of that advertising campaign.
Disadvantages	You may attract people who can only afford the reduced price and then are unable to continue training with you at the end of the discount period, even if they really liked it. Also, you want to ensure that you do not alienate any existing customers through promotions that you are offering to new ones.

Distributing leaflets

These can be fairly cheap to produce, particularly if you are able to do the design work yourself. The major cost of leafleting is often associated with the actual distribution. If you have access to a printer, you can consider printing the leaflets yourself. However, you will need to give consideration to the cost of the paper and ink, as well as the quality that you can produce.

Alternatively, you could find a printing company that could do the printing and maybe even the design for you. If you are thinking about doing a big print run, it is well worth looking into getting quotes for having the leaflets professionally printed. You will also probably end up with a far higher quality than you could manage at home. It can sometimes work out very cost effective to professionally print a much larger print run, but make sure that the design and content that you use will be relevant for, say, a couple of years, so that you don't have to do any more printing for a while.

Leaflets can contain specific information about your business and maybe even include a coupon to attract new customers to you. They can also be easily handed out to people who ask about your business or come along to try it out. Some further examples of things that you might put in a leaflet are:

- **Branding and logo**
- **Contact information**
- **Inspirational image**
- **Inspirational statement**
- **Some kind of demonstration of your uniqueness**
- **Training benefits**
- **Training times and location**

If you need to produce any registration, health check or assessment forms, you could use a lot of the same skills needed for developing leaflets to prepare your own branded forms that match the quality and image of your business.

Table 9.8: Distributing leaflets

Description	One-sided or two-sided leaflets that you design and distribute.
Why it works for sports and fitness businesses	Leaflets are great to leave in places where people are likely to be looking for information about sports and fitness services. Sports centres, health centres, community centres and schools are potential places to distribute your leaflets.
Cost	This can be quite expensive, especially if you are doing your own printing in colour with lots of images.

Advantages	You can always have something that you give to customers so that they don't leave empty-handed.
Disadvantages	If you distribute yourself, it can be both time-consuming and tiring. If you pay for someone else to distribute for you, it can be quite expensive.

Putting up posters

If you have somewhere appropriate to put posters up to promote your business, this can be very cost effective. If you are working through a local sports or fitness centre, you may be able to put posters up around the venue to try to attract business from the people who already use the venue for other things. Make sure that your posters are placed where there is a lot of passing footfall so that they have the best chance of being seen. Ideally a poster, in its simplest form, should be composed of an image, some text and your branding. It should be:

- **eye-catching**
- **simply designed**
- **brief and to the point**

Make sure you have posters up where you run your business, and also try to find other areas that will allow you to place your posters where they would be appropriate. Generally, the bigger the poster the better. You can print them at home on A4 sheets of paper or, for a more professional look, go for an A3 size or larger and get them professionally printed.

Table 9.9: Putting up posters

Description	Large format posters to place on display boards, which will easily and quickly attract attention to your business.
Why it works for sports and fitness businesses	Sports and health centres could be great places to attract new customers with well-designed and sensibly placed posters. They can also help you to build a presence where you operate.
Cost	Low cost if you print at home. If you get them printed professionally, it can be costly.

Advantages	Great longevity of your marketing material. Unlike leaflets you probably won't need to worry about checking up on the posters and whether you need to replace them.
Disadvantages	Some people find it really difficult to design posters. If you have trouble, make sure you look around at other ones and get feedback on your design before you commit to printing – even if that means asking your current customers.

Offering product samples and taster lessons

Remember that a lot of people like to try before they buy, or even try before they commit to taking on a new activity. You should ensure that you design your programme so that there is a clear entry point for new beginners, where you understand and cater for the fact that they are just trying out your activity. You should also ensure that there is a clear process of how they can proceed from there if they decide that they wish to continue with you.

A sample or taster lesson gives your new customers the confidence that there will be other people there who will be doing the same thing and that they won't be among far more advanced or able customers. This can reduce the barrier that they feel towards giving your coaching service a go. However, you will need to think carefully about how you will market these lessons, and also ensure that you do not lose money if you do not have enough people book in. You could think about whether there was some way that you could offer sample lessons at the same time and in the same venue as you carry out your normal coaching. This could help you to control the costs as well as making it easier for you to not worry about cancelling venues if you don't get enough people booked in. After all, you were going to be there at that time anyway because of your normal training.

Table 9.10: Offering product samples and taster lessons

Description	You could design specific training sessions that are for new customers and those people just wanting to try out your sport.
Why it works for sports and fitness businesses	This is another way of providing a low-risk option for people to try out your business.
Cost	There will obviously be the time that you spend, but there may also be equipment or venue hire costs that you will also need to take into account in your calculations.

Advantages	Attracts new customers to attend or start at the same time.
Disadvantages	You may have to run sample classes in isolation from your normal activities. There may be a cost associated with them and you may expend marketing effort but still not get people booked in.

Building your brand

Branding can take a number of different forms. It isn't just about creating a logo or picking a sound bite or punchline. Your business will have a brand right from the start, whether or not you consciously decide upon one. You yourself may even be the brand. Branding can be used to great effect to create an identity for your business and to unify all of your marketing efforts. You should ensure that your brand is on all the marketing materials that you create and use.

You don't have to spend lots of money on creating a brand. You can brainstorm and try to come up with some ideas with your family and friends. As long as it is catchy and distinctive, and reflects your business well, it should work for you. If you struggle coming up with a design, just try to think of a name that you are comfortable with and then perhaps pick an interesting font and colour that reflects your business. That way, you are keeping it simple and yet still trying to harness the power of branding. Remember that you don't have to get it perfectly right first time. As your business develops, you may get other ideas for branding your business or for improving your brand.

Table 9.11: Building your brand

Description	Some mark, name or visual way of identifying and differentiating your business.
Why it works for sports and fitness businesses	A sports or fitness business is just like any other business and, particularly since you are marketing directly to customers rather than to businesses, it can really help to have a distinct brand that people can remember and that you can potentially put on any merchandising in the future.
Cost	None if you create your brand yourself.

Advantages	Creates a way in which you can make all of your marketing work together and complement each other.
Disadvantages	You may find it difficult to come up with ideas for developing your brand identity. If so, you should look at how your competitors have branded themselves and what type of branding other businesses have used that appeals to you, which might help you to come up with ideas of your own.

Summary

Table 9.12 summarises entry-level traditional marketing techniques, ranging from using photography skills to building your brand. After reviewing these techniques, have a go at exercise 9.1. Make notes on whether you think that a particular marketing technique would be useful to you and how you could use it.

Table 9.12: Summary of entry-level traditional marketing techniques

MARKETING METHOD	DESCRIPTION
Using your photography skills	Sports and fitness training really lends itself to using lots of pictures in your marketing material. Creating a portfolio of digital pictures will mean that you have your own set of stock images that you can use as and when you please.
Using your computer skills	You could save a lot of time and money if you are proficient at using word processors, presentation software or even graphics packages to quickly create your own marketing materials.
Using your design skills	If you have an eye for good design and are a creative person, you may be able to draw upon this skill to come up with eye-catching and effective marketing materials.
Getting referrals from family and friends	Asking family and friends to recommend two or three people each, whom you could contact to give more information about your services, can be an easy way to get business when you have just started up.
Getting listed in directories	Listings in, for example, the Yellow Pages, the business pages and other relevant directories, including online directories, can be a cheap and effective way of reaching a large number of people in the local area.

Advertising	This is advertising that you pay for and includes adverts in the media. This can be one of the most expensive ways of marketing when you are starting up in business but also one of the quickest. It can be effective if it reaches the right people in the location that you are serving.
Offering coupons and discounts	This covers offering reduced-price, or even free, training sessions to attract customers. You'll need to be clear about the costs involved to you for offering such promotions and whether it is sustainable.
Distributing leaflets	Basic leaflets can be fairly cheap to produce, particularly if you do the design work and printing yourself, but printing colour versions may be quite expensive. The cost of leafleting is often associated with the actual distribution, which can be both time-consuming and tiring.
Putting up posters	Promoting your business this way can be very cost effective and attract lots of business, especially if you work in a local sports or fitness centre and can put posters up around the venue.
Offering product samples and taster lessons	By doing this, you provide a low-risk way for people to try before they buy. In particular, it allows beginners to try out an activity before making a commitment.
Building your brand	Branding is a mark, name or visual way of identifying your business that can be used to great effect on your marketing materials.

Exercise 9.1: Make notes on the usefulness to you of each entry-level marketing technique.

MARKETING TECHNIQUE	YOUR NOTES
Using your photography skills	
Using your computer skills	
Using your design skills	
Getting referrals from family and friends	
Getting listed in directories	
Advertising	
Offering coupons and discounts	
Distributing leaflets	
Putting up posters	
Offering product samples and taster lessons	
Building your brand	

CHAPTER 10
INTERMEDIATE TRADITIONAL MARKETING TECHNIQUES

Once you have got started with marketing and have put in place some simple marketing techniques that can have an immediate impact and are relatively quick to do, you can then start to look into slightly more advanced marketing techniques, which tend to be more time-consuming. They will help you to build your reputation and also to make you look more professional. You can build the reputation of your business using a number of different methods including writing articles about it, as well as looking for more creative ways of promoting your business.

Using your writing skills

If you are comfortable writing your own marketing material, you can save yourself a lot of time and potentially money normally spent on getting your ideas into a marketable form. Being able to write in a way that is appropriate for marketing your services is an excellent basic skill that can be used for developing all kinds of marketing material. You can write your own leaflets, brochures and posters. However, you can take this a step further by writing articles for local papers and even for magazines that are relevant to your coaching business. For those of you who are serious writers, you could consider writing your own coaching material in the form of booklets or even books, which you can use to promote your business both to your current customers and to future ones.

Having prepared all kinds of written material, you will then be able to pull something together very quickly if you have to. When you run demonstrations or taster sessions, you will have leaflets and brochures and even information packs ready to hand out. For your more regular students, you can think about whether there is anything that you can develop which would help to support and supplement their training with you. This could take the form of a written booklet that explains in words and pictures:

- **what you are coaching and your own individual approach and ideas;**
- **your thoughts on which aspects of what you teach are important;**
- **any other interesting facts you know of that you can share in a more systematic way.**

Always a good place to start is to look at what is already out there in terms of style of writing and the type of material that others have prepared. You do not have to limit your research to the specific area within which you are working. You should look for good ideas wherever you find them and then think about what might be appropriate for your business. Looking at what your direct competitors do may well be a good place to start. But don't limit yourself to what they try to do, as you may get the same results and fight over the same people. By using different methods of marketing you can potentially reach many more customers than your competitors.

If you feel that writing isn't your strength, you may still be able to develop great marketing materials by improving your awareness of what simple things work in other people's marketing, and learning to apply those techniques to your own business. This should help you to develop your own skills. You don't have to be a great writer to write effective marketing. You have to be far more aware of what approach will work for your target customers.

Writing is a general skill and if you are comfortable at developing your own marketing material, and are not afraid of having to work on it again and again over time to improve it, this can pay dividends. Most types of marketing that are relevant will require some form of written material and, since you are likely to be working alone, this is something that you may well have to try your hand at anyway. Leaflets, posters, articles and websites can all help to pull in customers for you. The more comfortable you are with writing your own material, the more marketing material you will be able to develop yourself which will help your business to grow. In addition, you won't have to worry about any copyright issues and, although writing may take up a lot of time, it certainly should not take up a lot of money.

It is always possible to get professional marketing material written and designed for you. But this costs money and you will still have to provide quite a lot of input because nobody knows your business like you do, and so it can still be quite time-consuming.

Table 10.1: Using your writing skills

Description	This includes writing for your brochures, website, articles, newsletters and even books.
Why it works for sports and fitness businesses	Almost all marketing material will require some form of writing and, since sports and fitness professionals may be working on their own, this will be a skill that will be really valuable.
Cost	The only real cost is time if you can write your own material.

Advantages	This will enable you to develop and try out relatively quickly a number of different marketing techniques.
Disadvantages	It can be time-consuming and you may not be comfortable about having to make that sacrifice in addition to the time that you already spend actually coaching. Also, if writing is not really for you, then you may find it quite difficult and painful to have to sit down with a blank piece of paper and try to come up with what to say.

Using direct mail

This is where you would actually send leaflets or brochures direct through the mailbox. A lot of advertising is done in this way and many households regularly receive such marketing mail shots. This marketing method can be an excellent way for a sports or fitness professional to market in the area local to their business. Most people who look for coaching will tend to search in the immediate local environment first. It is only when people start looking for very specialised sports and fitness services, or coaching for activities that are quite uncommon, that they are willing to travel that bit further. You need to understand whether your business is likely to appeal mostly to local people or to people over a much larger geographic area. Once you know that, you can focus on targeting your direct mail campaign.

Whatever you are planning to send as part of your direct mail campaign, you will need to have a mailing list to send it to. You can either look into creating your own mailing lists or you can purchase them, often from the postal service directly. However, purchasing mailing lists can be expensive and so you need to be very careful that you are clear about exactly what you want and what you are purchasing.

A cheaper way of distributing direct mail material is to either arrange for it to be added as an insert in a local paper or go and deliver the material door to door yourself. If you are unsure whether direct mailing will work for your business, you may first want to try a small run, where you create the leaflets and distribute them yourself.

Have an idea of how you will measure success, and, if you find that your trial was successful, you could look into trying a larger campaign with perhaps professionally printed material. In order to encourage people to act on your direct mail, you could think about including some kind of time-limited offer that would encourage people to try out your coaching. It could be a reduced-price lesson or even a free lesson. This will then make it easier for you to track whether your campaign worked and what your success rate was in terms of people who contacted you as a result of this method of promotion. If you decide to try this route, make sure that you have a realistic idea of how many customers you would need to generate using this method to break even on the cost of the direct-mail campaign. If you get your numbers, marketing and targeting right, direct mail can be very effective.

Table 10.2: Using direct mail

Description	This is sending letters, proposals or leaflets direct to the mailboxes of people on a mailing list.
Why it works for sports and fitness businesses	Many people look for coaching first within the local area. For this reason, depending on what your target market is, this technique could be an easy way to generate some new customers.
Cost	It can be a very expensive way of advertising. You would typically have to pay for the preparation and production of your marketing material, and you may also have to pay for a mailing list and distribution.
Advantages	For local businesses, this can be an excellent and quick way to generate some new customers.
Disadvantages	Can be both costly and time-consuming.

Creating brochures

These are sometimes hugely underrated. They are very versatile types of marketing and are essential for all coaching businesses.

Types of brochure

Brochures can take many different forms and you can use them in many different ways.

1. To briefly summarise your coaching offering

If you are an expert in what you are coaching, it is often easy to overlook that a new customer or student will not know as much about your training as you do. A mini-brochure that focuses on new customers and answers the kinds of question that they are most likely to ask, as well as providing background information that they may find inspiring, will help them to make a decision to train with you. On the one hand, this style of brochure will be uniquely targeted at them. On the other hand, if you are busy with other customers when new customers come to speak with you, then having all this information written down in a form that they can take away will make it easier for you to serve them. It will also make you look more professional as well as helping you stand out from the crowd. Brochures can have an extended shelf life, in that they may lie around a customer's home for a long time, all the while potentially promoting your business for you.

2. To supplement your coaching given in lessons
A second example is a brochure or booklet that supplements your coaching and is an excellent way to provide valuable material for your customer, while at the same time forming a great way of promoting your business. Many sports and fitness professionals tend to be worried about giving away the unique information and knowledge that they have built up through many years of training. You may also feel that, by writing down what you are teaching, you will somehow devalue your actual practical coaching. In fact, you are likely to find that the opposite is true. People learn in different ways, and giving your students an opportunity to think about what you are teaching, outside of the lesson and without trying to be physically active at the same time, may mean that they can understand certain things better that way. If you teach different types of class or aim your coaching at different levels of student, you could perhaps also use this as a way of developing a series of booklets that you could charge for, and thus add to your product range.

3. To present a guide to your services for different types of customer
A third type of brochure that you could consider is one that targets certain types of customer. If you find that your customers tend to fall into a number of distinct categories, you may feel that there is value in having brochures which answer the questions that those particular groups are likely to ask. If you have many different types of coaching service on offer, you might want to have a different selection aimed at different groups, or even market the same services in different ways to different groups.

4. To describe your range of products
You could prepare a small brochure that contains information about any products that you offer, along with a price list and an order form. You could design it to contain pictures of your products and highlight your recommendations for different types of student. For example, perhaps you have products that are particularly relevant to beginners, adults or children.

5. To offer other information to customers
Having now looked at four possible types of brochure, you can see that there is a lot of information that you could be providing in this way to your

customers. If you currently rely on giving all of this information verbally to each and every customer yourself, you have probably already run into some of the problems listed below:

- **Accidentally giving wrong or out-of-date information**
- **Failing to give relevant information**
- **Forgetting what you have already said to whom**
- **Neglecting to collect all relevant information from current and prospective students**

This is really important if you are working on your own, as appropriate brochures can help you to manage your workload and ensure that your customers do not suffer because you are overwhelmed with customer queries at the start and end of your coaching sessions. You can keep a selection of these in your coaching bag, perhaps in a folder that contains all of your other marketing material. You can then distribute or sell them as appropriate when needed.

Having a selection of brochures that support all the information you would like your customers to have at different stages of their relationship with your business will really cut down on how much you have to remember on the spot. In addition, all of these materials will help to generate extra sales for you and will speak on your behalf. They will also help you to stand out from the crowd and look more professional. They can even form materials that your students can hand to family and friends who may be interested, and so go on to support the promotion of your business in more ways than you might be able to imagine.

Table 10.3: Creating brochures

Description	These are small booklets that contain information about your training or your business.
Why it works for sports and fitness businesses	They are an excellent way to market your business and are really underused in the sports and fitness industry. So get your materials in place and start to see how they can generate sales on your behalf, while also making life easier for you.
Cost	You may find it time-consuming to produce them, so try to design the content in a way that is less likely to need updating over time. You can then print them out as and when you need them.

Advantages	Can reduce your workload. Excellent if you hate having to sell things personally and verbally. Give your business a professional feel and let them sell on your behalf.
Disadvantages	Potentially time-consuming to produce and the information contained within them may need regular updating.

Generating free publicity

There are many ways in which you can get free publicity. If you learn to look out for opportunities and take advantage of them when they arise, you can often create a good network that will generate such opportunities for you again in the future. Examples include:

- **Creating or taking part in newsworthy events**
- **Taking part in local events relevant to your business**
- **Offering free demonstrations and taster sessions at events**

Take the first example of creating newsworthy events. If you are a sports coach, have you got enough students to consider setting up your own regular competitions? Do your students take part in external competitions, or are they perhaps training with you to compete at regional or national level? You could use competition results from your sports coaching business to help to promote yourself – in the same way that schools use the exam results of their students to promote themselves.

If you don't think there are any ways of creating newsworthy events yourself, you could look into taking part in, or helping out with, somebody else's newsworthy event in return for your business being mentioned or promoted through that event. You may even find that this is a powerful way to make use of the marketing efforts of other organisations. You don't have to think about working just with other sports and fitness businesses to generate free publicity. You may be able to take part in the events of local organisations or communities, or even businesses that are promoting a completely different product or service which has the same target market as yourself.

Taking part in free publicity can also be an excellent way in which to improve your network. It may even be that some of these events are run annually and that, by building a good relationship, you will have access to that form of free publicity each year. See if there are any events that are run at your local shopping centre or sports centre, for example, that may be worthwhile your taking part in.

When an opportunity to get some free publicity comes along, it can be good to have some set pieces ready so that you can take advantage of opportunities that arise even at short notice. Having leaflets and brochures ready will mean that you have written material which you can easily reuse for the free publicity event. If you need to provide a demonstration, having some set demonstrations prepared that are designed for people who don't know much about your sports or your fitness training style can mean that you have something that is well rehearsed and ready to go at very short notice. If you have posters that you have been using for a while, you also have them ready to be used if there are opportunities for putting them up somewhere. You may be offered a stall or a booth at an exhibition-type event, and having lots of marketing material already designed and ready to use can ensure that you make the most of any free publicity opportunities that arise.

A word of warning, though, about free publicity – it can still be time-consuming and so after the event you will need to assess whether the return on the time and effort that you put in actually paid off. If it didn't, think twice before you agree to take part in a similar event again. Could your efforts have been better focused elsewhere?

Table 10.4: Generating free publicity

Description	Sometimes it is possible to generate free publicity through taking part in local events and offering free demonstrations and taster lessons. This can be an excellent way to sign up potential customers and access a part of the market on a scale that you would find difficult to reach alone.
Why it works for sports and fitness businesses	There can often be events run locally that you may be able to get involved in without having to pay, but instead offering perhaps a free demonstration or filling up a promotional booth or stall for the event organisers. This can be an excellent way to reach your target market.
Cost	If you have your marketing materials all ready to use, the cost can just be limited to your time and effort and possibly any production of sufficient materials to cover the event.
Advantages	It's free and could reach your target market.
Disadvantages	You may put in a lot of time and not come away with any new customers. Be careful about spending any money on such an event yourself – it can be really difficult to predict whether it will result in any new customers for you.

Getting word-of-mouth referrals

Word of mouth is one of the best ways of getting new business. If your current customers are so pleased with your coaching that they praise your efforts in front of friends and relatives, it can act as a way of their independently promoting your business. So simply keep your customers happy and they are more likely to sing your praises in the future. However, it may take quite some time for this method to start delivering new customers to you.

There are ways, though, in which you can speed this process up. For instance, you could:

- **provide incentives to your customers for making referrals;**
- **create specific free classes that your customers can recommend people to;**
- **provide time-limited coupons to your customers that they can hand out to friends.**

Each of these methods can act as a way to encourage your current customers or students to direct new customers to you. You could perhaps offer a free lesson to your student and their referral when they turn up with somebody. Or you could offer your student some kind of a discount or a training booklet if you have created one. There are many ways in which you may be able to incentivise your students without its actually costing you anything. You could even consider creating a special free beginners' class to which current students can make referrals. Another thing that you could try is handing out coupons for free lessons that your students can pass on to other people whom they think might be interested.

The key to helping along the generation of word-of-mouth referrals is to have some form of regular and predictable way in which your students can refer new customers to you. The reason why it has to be repeatable, predictable and regular is that your customers won't necessarily think of somebody to recommend when you first mention it to them. However, by having a regular mechanism in place to remind them that you do have some special offers aimed specifically at referrals will help them to help you. Therefore, when they do come across somebody who is appropriate for them to refer to you, they will know that you are open to their referrals and also how to go about doing it. It may surprise you, but it is not always obvious to customers that you would like them to refer people to you. By having a visible method to help with this, you will make it easier for them to do so. After all, why wouldn't you?

Table 10.5: Getting word-of-mouth referrals

Description	Encouraging your customers to refer people to you is one of the best ways of getting new customers. This method works best when people speak well of your business and want to promote you.
Why it works for sports and fitness businesses	Coaching is a very personal service – you work directly with your customers or your students, and over time they will get to know you and like how you coach them. This kind of relationship-based business is ideal for benefiting from word-of-mouth referrals.
Cost	Potentially no cost at all.
Advantages	Your own customers can become your strongest promoters and they will often be happy to refer customers to you, so that others may benefit from your coaching services.
Disadvantages	You mustn't push people to refer customers to you. It can even put your current customers off.

Using customer testimonials

Collecting testimonials from your customers is an easy way to generate information that you can use in all kinds of marketing material from leaflets and brochures to posters and websites. Testimonials are simply statements or phrases that your customers use to perhaps describe your business and their experience with it. One easy way to collect information that you could use in testimonials is by having a questionnaire that you could ask your students to fill in. You could ask a number of questions that are likely to generate the kind of information you would be able to use in your own marketing. For example:

- **What first made you interested in joining these classes?**
- **What do you like about the training?**
- **What do you like about the atmosphere of the group?**
- **How does the training influence other aspects of your life?**
- **What benefits have you received from the training that have surprised you?**
- **What are the reasons why you prefer these classes to others that you have tried?**

You can then use this feedback in various forms in your marketing. Testimonials give a real face to your business – they can show potential customers how other people have found your coaching or your classes. It can make it easier for them to approach you to try the lessons because they feel that they can better associate with you through the testimonials that they see.

If you have celebrities who come to train with you, consider asking them for a testimonial about your business that you could use in your marketing materials. Although celebrity endorsements can be more powerful in attracting new business than other types of testimonial, they can all serve to help build the brand and image of your business as well as giving it a face that new customers can trust and be inspired by.

Table 10.6: Using customer testimonials

Description	These are short comments from your customers that praise your business.
Why it works for sports and fitness businesses	Coaching is a very personal service business. Testimonials can help potential customers create a link to your business through people like them who have come to train with you.
Cost	Only that of putting the questionnaires together and then processing the information.
Advantages	They can provide a way for potential customers to see how others have found and benefited from your coaching. They can potentially be used in all of your marketing materials and can give a friendly and inde-pendent face to your business.
Disadvantages	Not everybody will be comfortable about giving testimonials.

Running demonstrations

It can be worthwhile having a set demonstration or even a few of them. They can be designed to last different amounts of time, to target various markets and to demonstrate key parts of your service offering. You can then use them either as material during your coaching or when you pitch for business with new customers or organisations, and you would have something ready to go if you get invited at short notice to local events to give demonstrations or to exhibit. Remember that demonstrations are aimed at an audience different from your normal students, who may already know quite a lot about you, and so you will need to take that into account when developing your material.

When preparing your demonstration you need to ensure that it is suitable for your audience. For a demonstration that is aimed at beginners, you may want to include some of the following:

- **A short verbal introduction about your training**
- **Some background about your sport or training style**

- Some of the things that new students might do when they first start
- Something inspirational that more advanced students would be able to do
- An opportunity for the audience to ask you questions
- The distribution of relevant leaflets or booklets that accompany the demonstration

Table 10.7: Running demonstrations

Description	A set piece that demonstrates some aspect of your sports or fitness training. This would probably be aimed at people who are completely new to your sport or training.
Why it works for sports and fitness businesses	Demonstrations are an excellent way for sports and fitness businesses to generate interest and attract customers, and also to reinforce to your current customers why they should continue training with you.
Cost	For most sports and fitness professionals, it should be possible to create some form of demonstration without incurring any additional cost. If you need to use equipment or special clothing, you probably already have this as part of your coaching business.
Advantages	Once you have created a set demonstration, it can be very easy for you to give a smooth demonstration at short notice. You can potentially make it entertaining for new and current customers alike.
Disadvantages	It can be time-consuming to put together a demonstration and you may not feel comfortable performing in front of people. If you are nervous, it may be worthwhile working with one of your students in doing the demonstration.

Summary

Table 10.8 summarises intermediate traditional marketing techniques, ranging from using your writing skills to running demonstrations. After reviewing these techniques, have a go at exercise 10.1. Make notes on whether you think that a particular marketing technique would be useful to you and how you could use it.

Table 10.8: Summary of intermediate traditional marketing techniques

MARKETING METHOD	DESCRIPTION
Using your writing skills	This is a valuable skill required in almost all marketing materials and includes writing for your brochures, articles in newspapers and magazines, newsletters, website pages, and even books.
Using direct mail	If you have a mailing list, you could consider sending letters, brochures or leaflets using the postal service. A cheaper way is to distribute them as inserts in newspapers and magazines, or by door-to-door leafleting.
Creating brochures	These are small booklets that contain information to give to both existing and potential customers. Some typical uses are to describe your products and services or to supplement your coaching.
Generating free publicity	It may be possible to generate free publicity by taking part in local or news-worthy events and offering free demon-strations and taster lessons. This can be an excellent way to target a wider market and sign up potential customers.
Getting word-of-mouth referrals	Word-of-mouth referrals can be slow to deliver results but offering incentives to your existing customers can encourage them to refer people to you and can bring in new business quite quickly.
Using customer testimonials	Endorsements from past and present customers are ideal for promoting confi-dence in your business to potential clients. They can be used in all types of marketing material, for example in your leaflets and brochures, and on your website pages.
Running demonstrations	You can design set demonstrations for different requirements such as pitching for business or complementing your coaching. Among other things, they are useful for generating interest in your products and services.

Exercise 10.1: Make notes on the usefulness to you of each intermediate marketing technique.

MARKETING TECHNIQUE	YOUR NOTES
Using your writing skills	
Using direct mail	
Creating brochures	
Generating free publicity	
Getting word-of-mouth referrals	
Using customer testimonials	
Running demonstrations	

CHAPTER 11
ADVANCED TRADITIONAL MARKETING TECHNIQUES

Once you have made a start with marketing and put in place some simple marketing techniques from earlier chapters, you can begin to consider whether some of the more advanced marketing techniques are suitable for your business. In many respects, the marketing techniques described in this chapter are more appropriate for a slightly more established business where you have a good idea about the coaching services and products that you offer and perhaps have some branding in place, and are looking to develop your reputation, enhance your professionalism and potentially attract a much wider audience to your business to help it to grow.

The emphasis is on marketing techniques that develop your intellectual assets through the creation of a range of products which you can sell, and which at the same time promote your business for you. Up until now you would have paid for your marketing with money, time and effort. Advanced marketing techniques enable you to share some of the cost of marketing your business with your customers and potential customers, while also providing them with a valuable product. Executed correctly, this can be an extremely effective way of marketing your business in a really professional manner.

Of course, the drawback to these marketing techniques is that they can be very time-consuming indeed to put into place. Writing a book or developing a professional quality DVD can be really hard work and take a lot of time. In addition, you may even have to pay for some parts of the development that you are unable to do yourself. Once you start developing products that you can sell and that also promote your business, you may well start coming up with other ideas about what you could try. The main thing to remember is that you always need to weigh up the cost in time and effort on your behalf with the potential benefit from the activity. Ideally, you may want to try developing something on a small scale that you can produce yourself, and see whether it generates enough interest to justify your going ahead with a full-scale project.

Using your creativity

Coaching requires creativity in order to teach the same material to different types of people and also to keep it interesting for them and for you. Coaches tend to have a large amount of knowledge that they tap into as and when required. Through using your creativity, you have the potential to start creating some products based purely on your ideas. It can be extremely satisfying to see a creative project through from start to finish. Products such as books, DVDs and merchandise are an excellent way for you to utilise your creativity and knowledge if you are able to.

Table 11.1: Using your creativity

Description	Coming up with ideas and turning them into reality.
Why it works for sports and fitness businesses	A lot of the coaching knowledge that you already have is likely to be excellent material for bringing together into some form of product.
Cost	Apart from the cost of your time and effort in the development of these intellectual assets, there will be the additional cost of production.
Advantages	You should find it really rewarding to see the end products such as books, DVDs and merchandise.
Disadvantages	Will require you to remain focused over long periods of time during development, with little in terms of being able to see immediately the effect on your business.

Writing books

In chapter 10 we looked at brochures and mini-booklets that you could provide to your customers. You can take this one step further and think about putting together a more substantial piece of work. You may have noticed that a number of sports and fitness books are indeed written by sports and fitness professionals. What do you think about the books that are already out there which touch upon your area? Do you feel that you have some unique perspective or teaching style that would be useful to have in writing, both for your current students and for potential new students? Do you think that the books you have seen enhance the reputation and professionalism of the people who wrote them? Can you imagine that such a book helps to set that particular sports or fitness professional apart from others in their field? Would you yourself be excited about training with someone who had released their own book in your field of interest?

Like brochures and booklets, books targeted appropriately can be excellent marketing tools. They can help to set your business apart from any other and provide your students with a compelling and unique reason to train with you. The great thing is that you only have to write it once. Writing a book in any form is a substantial and long-term commitment. It can be really easy to come up with an idea for a book but far harder to actually get it written. If successful, the book itself may form a product that you can sell to bring in an additional income stream for your business. Since writing can be hard work, it is best to ensure that this is something you will enjoy doing in its own right. You cannot guarantee the benefits from such a project and on its own, and without a sound business proposition to back it up, it may be time spent unwisely.

Once you have written a book, there are many ways in which you could get it produced, and you should have a good idea in your mind about how you will do so before you make a start on actually writing. Examples include:

- **Printing at home**
- **Making an e-book**
- **Self-publishing by sending to a short-run books printer**
- **Creating a print-on-demand book**
- **Publishing through a reputable publisher**

The next question then is what to put in the book? Luckily, as a sports or fitness professional there are probably loads of things that you could think of which would be appropriate. If you are coaching people all the time, and also have taken students in as beginners and trained them all the way to an advanced level, you probably have a wealth of information that you could consider as material for your book. Take for example:

- **Instructions for beginners**
- **Background or history of your sport or fitness training area**
- **Lesson plans**
- **Exercises**
- **Tactics**
- **Your own teaching methods**

Once you start to consider what knowledge you have that you routinely share without thinking about it, you may begin to realise that you do indeed have a lot of information which is worth sharing. You should not feel that you are devaluing your coaching by getting this information written down.

The other added bonus that sports and fitness professionals have in terms of preparing material for their books is that a lot of what they do is very visual. Therefore, there are plenty of opportunities for having very attractive and visually stimulating books presenting your information through a combination of words and pictures. Since books are so much work, and because there is no guarantee about the effect that they will have on your business, you will find that this can be an excellent way to make you completely stand out from your competitors. A lot of other people may be put off even by thinking about the amount of effort required to complete such a project. It can help to firmly establish you as an expert in your field and form one of the easiest answers to prospective students on why they should train with you.

Table 11.2: Writing books

Description	Capturing your knowledge in some form of book can help to strengthen your business.
Why it works for sports and fitness businesses	The coaching business is very visual and coaches tend to have a wealth of knowledge, an ideal combination for creating a book. If you are also a keen writer, putting together a book could be a worthwhile long-term project.
Cost	Extremely expensive in terms of time. If you plan to print the book yourself, that may also cost quite a bit. There are some cheaper options in the forms of e-book or print-on-demand book.
Advantages	Firmly establishes you as an expert in your field, makes you completely stand out from all of your competition and shows your students what you have to offer.
Disadvantages	You cannot guarantee the effect that a book will have on your business. It is a long-term commitment and it can be very hard work to see it through to the end.

Creating DVDs

Like books, DVDs really lend themselves to getting a message across for sports and fitness professionals. As discussed in the previous section, the coaching of sports and fitness programmes is very visual and for this reason it can make ideal material for producing DVDs. In fact, it may well be far easier for you to create a DVD than to write a book. You can think about including the same kind of material that was discussed in the previous section, ranging from instructions for beginners to your own teaching methods.

This time you need to be far more aware of how things look on camera. It can be very easy to create something that looks amateurish and could end up having a negative effect on your business. You may perhaps want to try making some short clips and seeing if your students find them useful. By doing this, you will be able to see what is involved in creating a DVD and what works on screen.

You will need to plan out what you intend to put on the DVD and think about how you will present the information. You don't want to pack too much information onto a single disk – perhaps you could create a series of DVDs. Remember that different people learn things in different ways and so a combination of your coaching, any material that you write and perhaps a range of DVDs to choose from can add value for your students and at the same time increase the value of your business through the development of intellectual assets. People will tend to buy DVDs that are generic to your area of expertise; however, if they could get something directly relevant to what you are teaching that has been developed by you, they are even more likely to purchase it from you.

If you are unsure about whether this is suitable for your business, have a look at what is already available to see if there is some unique angle that you have which would be a valuable addition to what is already out there. You can find DVDs through bookshops, including online bookshops such as Amazon. You could also take a look at the types of video that have been loaded onto YouTube. These can start to give you ideas of what kinds of thing you might want to include and also an indication of the types of video that are proving to be popular downloads.

DVDs can be cheaper to produce than books and so this marketing route is not to be lightly ignored. Also, having the option of distributing your video online or electronically means you can potentially bring the costs right down. Electronic distribution has the additional benefit that you don't have to worry about cover design for the DVD box or anything else that would be related to creating a physical copy. If you intend to produce the DVDs yourself at home, you can easily buy the blank disks and cases to do this. You could then design and print the cover and DVD labels yourself, especially if you have access to a high-quality colour laser printer. If you discover that your initial trials are successful, you may also think about mass producing and publishing your DVDs. You can find professional firms that can take care of all of that for you.

When producing the DVD, you should think carefully about whether you want to be the star of the video or whether you need to get a student to be in it so that you can watch and ensure that certain techniques or skills are correctly demonstrated and captured onto video. You may decide to use a combination of these two methods.

There are many advantages to creating video footage. This is because, just like any writing that you produce or any photographs that you take, it can be used in many different ways. You can use video to supplement all kinds of other marketing efforts, as well as creating a formal DVD that you may want to sell or distribute to your students in some way. You may also produce DVDs to give away at events, or to play during certain types of demonstration or exhibition, and as a way of sending samples of your coaching to potential clients, thereby saving you the effort and cost of a personal visit. You can even record short clips that you could post on your website so that people can sample your coaching before they come, and so help support their decision to come along and train with you.

The disadvantages of creating video are that, as in the case of writing a book, it can be very time-consuming and potentially costly to have done to a professional standard. It is also impossible to know exactly what impact it will have on your business and so it can be quite an investment on your part. However, the potential for using the material and creating something that your students will value can be very rewarding. Remember of course that you are also increasing the value of your business through creating further intellectual assets.

Table 11.3: Creating DVDs

Description	Taking video footage of, for example, some of your coaching, and packaging that into a DVD.
Why it works for sports and fitness businesses	Coaching and training people is an incredibly visual activity. This naturally lends itself to the creation of self-help and training-supplement types of video.
Cost	Luckily the attractive price of video equipment has now made it at least an option that individuals could consider in terms of borrowing equipment or purchasing their own to develop video material to support their business. You can keep costs down by distributing the video only in electronic format over the Internet. Producing physical copies may be a consideration once you have a better idea of how much benefit your business will receive from such activity.
Advantages	Develops another form of intellectual asset for your business that you will be able to use in many different ways to support your marketing efforts.
Disadvantages	Can be costly and time-consuming. Important to ensure that the quality of the end product is in line with the image of your business that you are trying to portray.

Developing your own merchandise

When you are developing your brand, it is good to keep in mind that you want it to be versatile enough to be used in many different ways. Merchandise is just one example of how you might like to use your brand to promote your business. Merchandise can take many different forms, for example clothing, pens and key rings. However, clothing is one of the types that is naturally well-suited to sports and fitness businesses. Most sports and fitness training will require some kind of special clothing. This can create opportunities for you to have clothing and equipment that is branded with your business. If your sport requires specific clothing, is there some way that you could add a badge representing your business? Or is there potential to create branded t-shirts and fleeces that you could offer to students? Either they could purchase these from you or you could include them in the price of joining your training group or registering with you. Branded clothing is a practical way of getting your business marketed for you by your customers. If you put details such as your website onto the clothing, you make it even easier for potential customers to get in touch with you.

You can then advertise branded clothing and equipment through your leaflets, brochures and websites if you have them. You can further promote your business by wearing the branded items yourself. This creates a very subtle way of marketing your business without having to actually say anything at all. You and others can then be marketing your business for you without even noticing. This kind of passive marketing can be quite effective, particularly if you are operating your business in a very localised area. If your students come and go to your sessions wearing your branded clothing and carrying your branded equipment, they will be sending a clear message wherever they go.

An issue with merchandise is that it is expensive and you don't want to order mass quantities of items only to find that you are unable to sell them. It is much better to identify a supplier who will allow you to do small quantities of branded items, so that you can order them once you have received firm customer orders and payments. Thus, you minimise the risk to your business while at the same time offering your customers an additional product that they could purchase from you.

There is still an upfront cost associated with designing the way in which any items will be branded, and also there is the time that is associated with finding a suitable supplier and getting in place a pricing deal. As long as you don't put any money in upfront until you have confirmed orders from customers, you should be able to ensure that you don't have to pay for the goods before you receive payment from your customers.

If you feel that it is a lot of hassle trying to sell clothing and equipment to your students, think about whether it is worthwhile bundling a t-shirt, say, with a membership package or a training session. Even if you absorb some of the cost of the item, remember that you are still creating value for your customer by giving them an item and they may well use it and generate free marketing for you.

Providing branded merchandise can, however, do so much more for you. Particularly for sports and fitness groups, wearing branded clothing is a way that people can show their interest, support and pride in the coaching that you are providing. Sports and fitness training often brings disparate groups of people together, creating an opportunity for making new friends and developing relationships. Your business could easily become the one thing that the people training with you have strongly in common. Remember that people tend to do sports and fitness training because they enjoy it, and that in itself will strengthen the value and reputation of your business. This can build a strong sense of community, and your branding and merchandise can be a visual acknowledgement of that.

Table 11.4: Developing your own merchandise

Description	Branded clothing and equipment is something that promotes your business and builds a sense of community.
Why it works for sports and fitness businesses	Most people training tend to need some form of kit and so developing your own merchandise could easily be integrated into your business.
Cost	You can minimise the cost to you by taking payments before you actually place the order for the items.
Advantages	A passive form of marketing that enhances the reputation of your business, attracts new customers and builds a sense of identity within your training group.
Disadvantages	Can be time-consuming to set up the initial design and find suppliers.

Summary

Table 11.5 summarises advanced traditional marketing techniques, ranging from using your creativity to developing your own merchandise. After reviewing these techniques, have a go at exercise 11.1. Make notes on whether you think that a particular marketing technique would be useful to you and how you think you could use it.

Table 11.5: Summary of advanced traditional marketing techniques

MARKETING METHOD	DESCRIPTION
Using your creativity	Developing intellectual assets will certainly draw upon your creativity and resourcefulness. These activities can be very time-consuming and are really intended for the much longer-term development of your business.
Writing books	Books can be an excellent way to attract new customers, strengthen the value of your services with your current customers and build the intellectual asset base of your business. They can also be an excellent marketing tool that you always have to hand, which you can both sell and hand out to prospective clients as appropriate. Everybody is happy to receive a free book.
Creating DVDs	Sports and fitness businesses are absolutely ideal for using DVDs as a promotional tool. You can demonstrate on DVD your coaching with perhaps a session teaching beginners, create a DVD of exercise or sport techniques, or even compose a whole range of DVDs.
Developing your own merchandise	Sports and fitness professionals are in a unique position where their students need to wear some kind of uniform or special sports clothes to take part in the activity. This creates an excellent opportunity for you to develop your own range of branded clothing such as branded kit, towels, t-shirts and fleece jackets.

Exercise 11.1: Make notes on the usefulness to you of each advanced marketing technique.

MARKETING TECHNIQUE	YOUR NOTES
Using your creativity	
Writing books	
Creating DVDs	
Developing your own merchandise	

CHAPTER 12
ELECTRONIC MARKETING TECHNIQUES

Websites, email and electronic newsletters are all examples of electronic marketing techniques. A well-thought-out website and process for managing it can be a powerful tool in your marketing portfolio. If you are uncomfortable with technology, it can be a little difficult knowing where to start. Without a clear idea of what you want to achieve from your electronic marketing efforts, it will not be easy to put something practical in place. Electronic marketing has the potential to be a relatively cheap channel that could bring you great results. You should remember to keep up to date with how data protection legislation affects any information that you are planning to process electronically as well as traditionally.

You don't have to be comfortable with using technology or computers yourself. If you have a clear idea of what you are trying to achieve, it is always possible to hire somebody to do the set-up for you. If you are comfortable using computers for sending emails and browsing the Internet, you can still develop a system that matches your skills.

Using more advanced computer skills
In chapter 9 we looked at making use of some basic computer skills that mostly involved using common off-the-shelf software. If you have more advanced computer skills, they too can be put to work. See if you are comfortable with any of the following:

- **Using email**
- **Browsing the Internet**
- **Purchasing online**
- **Using web-based software and wizards**
- **HTML programming to develop websites**
- **Database programming to develop more sophisticated websites**

As you go down the list, you can probably see that there is an increase in the computer ability required. If you do have any of these skills, you may well be able to use them to gain a competitive edge. The rest of this chapter looks at how you can use these advanced computer skills and also customer and member management systems to help market your business.

Table 12.1: Using more advanced computer skills

Description	Starting from basic email and Internet browsing skills, right the way through to developing your own website.
Why it works for sports and fitness businesses	More and more people look for information about what they can do, and where, on the Internet. Being comfortable with using this technology to your advantage can bring customers to you whom you would otherwise be unable to attract.
Cost	If you want to look into developing these skills yourself, it will take time and cost money for training courses for you to learn them. There may also be costs in terms of computer hardware/software, Internet connection and web hosting.
Advantages	Could speed up your ability to attract new customers and to serve current ones as well as giving you a competitive edge.
Disadvantages	Even if you do have these skills, it can still be time-consuming to put them to good use.

Using email and mailing lists

The most basic form of electronic marketing is to keep a mailing list of your customers in either a text document or a spreadsheet, and to use this for sending regular communications to your customers. You don't want to email too frequently, but you should equally avoid never communicating with your customers. You will need to find the right balance that suits both you and the people you are contacting. You can use emails to provide information about new products and services, to send vouchers or offers, or even to collect customer feedback. If you have a mailing list in place, you have the option of trying out new ideas on existing customers at little expense. You will need to have some system for managing your customer information, otherwise it can be difficult to add value for your customers and also to demonstrate your business offering.

What should be in my mailing list?

In the simplest form, your mailing list should have the names of your customers and their email addresses. Using a spreadsheet can be the easiest way, as you can use one column for the name and another for the email address. Alternatively, a two-column table in a text document can do the job just as well. You can then compose your email and use the list to send it out to people. You can do this by creating a group in your email client that contains all the email addresses, or you can use more sophisticated tools such as Microsoft Word and the 'Mail Merge' feature.

Table 12.2: Using email and mailing lists

Description	Creating a contact list for all of your customers to whom you can send out emails with relevant information.
Why it works for sports and fitness businesses	As the number of your customers grows, it will be very difficult for you to make sure that everybody has the latest information. Email will enable you to provide consistent and timely information.
Cost	None – if you already have email set up on your computer. Otherwise, the cost of an internet connection through a service provider.
Advantages	Low-cost way to get information to your customers in a professional manner.
Disadvantages	Your mailing list will need to be updated regularly.

Developing a website

Websites can do a great many things for your business. They can:

- **provide a place where people can go to find out more about you**
- **generate new enquiries and clients**
- **sell your products and services for you**
- **provide a platform to try out new product and service ideas**
- **add to your reputation and professionalism**

Websites can vary hugely in size and complexity, from a simple one-page website that just states what your business is and how people can get in touch, to an electronic shop that showcases all of your products and services to the world.

Do I need a website?

Having a website can greatly add to your reputation and it also serves as an informal place where people can go to find out more about you without having to ask you directly. People can use your website to form judgements about your business and to help them to decide whether they wish to train with you. If you are working independently and are strapped for time, then, used correctly, your website could drive new business to you.

What's involved in getting a website?

To set up a website, you would need the following:

- **Domain name (website address)**
- **Website hosting**
- **Website design**
- **Content and images**
- **Regular updating of information**

Once the initial work of getting a website in place is done, you need to think about often-neglected elements such as updating the website to keep it current and generating new content to keep it interesting. In the longer term, this can turn out to be quite time-consuming, and so it is essential to take into account what kind of updating you are likely to do and how frequently that might be.

How do I go about getting a website in place?

Having decided that a website fits well with your marketing objectives, you need to consider how you can go about getting this organised. This can be the challenging part. Some examples of how sports and fitness professionals have approached this task include:

1. Creating one yourself

You may have the skills for putting together websites yourself. If this is the case, you should certainly seriously consider having a website for your business. The advantages are that you should then have only website-hosting costs to cover. Designing good websites can be quite demanding and, if this isn't something that you are naturally good at, it may be difficult to make your website look good and work well.

2. Using offline website-design software

There are off-the-shelf software packages that you can buy and use to design your website. You will then still have to find some way of hosting your website. If you buy a bespoke website-design software package, don't forget that you will need to learn how to use it, and that can take time.

3. Using an online website-design tool

Some companies that provide website hosting also offer online tools that work like a software wizard to enable you to do some basic design work and add your own content to create simple websites. These normally require you to be paying a monthly subscription for your hosting. It may be difficult to obtain the exact look and feel that you want for your website, as you will be constrained by the website-designing tool's capabilities. On the other hand, this can be a very quick and efficient way to get a website in place, particularly if you prefer not to have to understand the technicalities. In most cases, this type of website will be fine to get you started. Once your business is up and running, you can always look into getting a more personalised website in place. By then, you will have a better idea of what works on your website and what you would like a more sophisticated website to do for you.

4. Asking a friend or relative to create one for you
You may be lucky enough to know somebody who has the skills and time to set up a website for you. This can certainly be a great place to start and should be a low-cost, or even free, option. You will still need to be clear about what you want your website to look like and you will have to provide all the content. This includes all the text, the design of the pages and any images that you would like on the website.

5. Hiring a website-design firm
This is likely to be the most expensive way in which to get your website in place. Here you use a professional website-design firm to design and implement your website, based on your requirements and specifications. Since this can be really expensive, it will be important to be absolutely clear about what you want the end result to be. Remember that the website-design firm will still need to be given information about your business and the text, and possibly even the images that you would like to be used.

6. Using a combination of methods
In practice, you may find that you end up using a mixture of these methods over time. The most difficult part can be getting started, but once you have something in place you can work on adding more features to it as appropriate and improve it over time.

What can I put on my website?
The easiest thing to do is to start with a simple layout and then work your way up in terms of complexity and content. Building a website can take time and so it's better to get something in place first and then add to it as your business develops.

1. Your business and contact information
The most important things to have on your website are information about your business, products and services, and how people can get in touch with you. This is probably the very least you should have, but an excellent place to start from for later showcasing and building your brand reputation.

2. Ability to contact you by filling in a form on your website

You might wonder why this is needed if you have already placed your contact information, including email address, on your website. In practice, not everyone likes to click on an email address and then use their email client to send a message to you. By having a form on your website that they can fill in online, you can make it easier for people to get in touch with you.

3. Selling your products and services online

Some people may like to contact you personally to arrange for coaching, but others may prefer the initial contact to be through a transaction on your website. For this reason, having the convenience for a customer to make an instant purchase can be a great addition to your website. It gives your customer the opportunity for some instant gratification. You know your website is successful and working well for your business when people are purchasing directly from there without having made any contact with you first. You could think about designing your services in a way that makes them suitable for online purchase: for example, having an introductory session at regular times throughout the year, or making available books or guides that you can sell directly and post to fulfil the order. Electronic shops are discussed in more detail later in this chapter.

4. Generating advertising revenue

You could even consider using your website to let other businesses have advertisement space that could generate revenue for you. Online advertising through Google Ads could be a good place to start, to see if this works for you and suits your website. Do remember, though, that some people may find the fact that you use your website for advertising third-party businesses unprofessional.

5. Customer management system

Probably the most complicated and expensive addition to your website can be that of a customer management system. This is a database management system that links into your website. In some cases, you may have parts of the system visible to your customers, for example a login to their account, or you may have the system set up so that only the administrator or manager of the website can see it. Back-end systems can be designed to:

- **add customers to a mailing list**
- **create an individual account area through a login**
- **monitor your customer relationships and manage your contact history**
- **generate electronic newsletters**

It is possible to buy solutions that can do some of these things for you; it is also possible to have a bespoke system designed, implemented and managed for you. A database system is particularly useful as the number of customers whom you are managing increases, since it provides a way for you still to have regular contact with them and to professionally manage the relationships. These systems can be excellent in terms of saving you time as well as boosting your business revenue and reputation.

The difficulty with such systems, however, is that they do need to be managed and require somebody to provide support and guidance when it is requested by customers. So, there can be an ongoing time or cost commitment involved. These tools are further discussed later in this chapter.

How do I sell my services and products online?

If you run courses or have classes or products that customers could purchase from you online, you could consider setting up some kind of shopfront on your website. You could then take bookings and payments directly through this electronic shop and, for products, have them either picked up directly from you or posted, or for services people could book in for particular classes or courses. You can even decide to take bookings online and then take payment in person when your client turns up for their session. Alternatively, there are several ways in which you can process online payments:

- **PayPal**
- **Google Checkout**
- **Request a bank transfer**
- **Request the completion of a downloadable form that can be posted to you with a cheque**

It may seem a little daunting to set up an electronic shop, but there are a number of ways that you can do this. You could try starting off with a simple version or a small pilot and then build on that over time. If successful, you can start thinking about how you could expand your offering and serve more people.

1. Creating your own electronic shop

If you are able to create your own website, it may be worthwhile having a go at putting together an online shop too. You could use any of the other methods described here, or you could consider just creating a web page that lists and describes your products and services and then adding some form of payment button, for example to use PayPal or Google Checkout. Or you could go for an even simpler option first – just accept bookings online and then leave taking payments to when you actually meet your client.

2. Using an electronic-shop wizard provided by website-hosting companies

Some website-hosting companies give you an option of setting up an electronic shop using their shop-generating wizard. This can be a good place to start, as it takes away a lot of the technical issues of developing your own design and so you can focus on your product and service range.

3. Setting up a virtual store on your website

If you don't want to manage the payment systems and detailed website-design work yourself, you could look into collaborating with other firms to provide a shopfront on your website.

4. Using a combination of methods

You might find that a mixture of these methods works best for you, depending on how well they match your range of products and services. If you are starting out as, say, a personal trainer, you can test your services by providing an online booking facility. Or, if you are a yoga instructor, for example, you could set up a website that offers online booking into the courses that you run each quarter. In this way, you could promote your courses well in advance and look to see whether a course was going to be successful enough to make it worthwhile running.

Table 12.3: Developing a website

Description	Having an online presence through a website that is dedicated to promoting your business.
Why it works for sports and fitness businesses	People are increasingly using the Internet and website searches in the same way that they use printed directories for finding local businesses and services.
Cost	Varies depending on the sophistication of the website.
Advantages	A 24-hour and 7-day-a-week promotional tool that markets your business and directs customers to you.
Disadvantages	Requires updating and can be costly.

Using electronic newsletters and magazines

Once you have put in place a website, you can increase its value to you if you have some way of sending out electronic newsletters or magazines that aim to entice customers back to your website. They can direct your customers to any new products, promotions and other relevant information.

You could even post your 'coming soon' events, stories, testimonials and so much more. The great thing about a newsletter is that it gives you your own forum for promoting new products and services, and trialling your new ideas on existing customers, the people who already know and trust you.

The frequency of your newsletter will be determined by what makes sense for your business. If you have a complicated schedule, with things that change every week, you may want to send out a weekly newsletter. If, on the other hand, your programme is fairly consistent throughout the year and you only need to let your customers know about closures, then just a quarterly newsletter might be enough. The difficult thing about newsletters and magazines is creating new content each time. Therefore, the frequency of your newsletter may be determined by how often you can generate new content. This can all seem like quite a lot of work, especially if you plan to do this yourself each week or each month.

You therefore need to look to see if you can make things easier for yourself. You can do this by making sure that you plan activities in advance. For example, from September onwards you may want to start putting together your programme for the following year. Having a programme outlined in front of you means you can then work to it to ensure that you always promote the events well in advance of their actual delivery. In this way, you can try to generate interest, and perhaps even bookings, in advance. If, for whatever reason, something that you were trying out doesn't look like it is going to be successful, you may even have time to make venue or other cancellations so that you don't lose any money. Having a plan can make a really big difference to how you can market yourself.

Which newsletter format to use?

A newsletter may take the form of a simple text email or you could create a more sophisticated media-enriched version. It is important that your recipients have the option to specify their choice of format if you plan to have different types available.

1. Simple text email

The easiest way to set up an electronic newsletter is to start with just simple text emails, in which you might also include a link to your website. Until you are comfortable with the idea of regularly generating content for a newsletter, you could try just sending a monthly or quarterly update. You can then use your mailing list to send out your text newsletter to your customers.

2. HTML newsletter

You might prefer to send out emails with graphics and links presented in a more user-friendly way. In fact, you may want the newsletter to look like a web page and for this you will probably need to use your website-hosting company. Once you can send HTML newsletters, you can start being more powerful with your marketing. For example, you can raise your brand awareness with your customers by having regular features and also the latest news. You could even think about including surveys and polls.

3. HTML newsletter combined with a customer management system

The most effective way to run regular newsletters is through some form of customer management system. This is basically a database that contains information such as your contact details and the history of what communications each customer has received. This kind of customer management system, combined with the ability to quickly build newsletters, can make it much easier to manage your customer relationships.

Table 12.4: Using electronic newsletters and magazines

Description	An electronic method of regularly keeping in touch with your customers.
Why it works for sports and fitness businesses	Your coaching programme may vary from week to week or from month to month. Having a way to communicate your programme to your customers means that you are more likely to keep their custom.
Cost	Varies depending on the sophistication of the system used.
Advantages	Means that there is less information that you have to remember to give students while you are coaching.
Disadvantages	Requires you to regularly create content.

Using customer management systems

A customer management system is simply a way in which you can manage your customer contact information. It enables you to keep track of your customers and the contact that you have with them. If you have a large number of customers and find it difficult to remember exactly what you have said or what you have sold to them so far, a customer management system can help you to better manage that relationship. A good system will also prompt you about what needs to be done next. It should keep track of your communications for you. For example, if you send out electronic newsletters, it should be able to track which ones each customer has received.

Such relationship management systems can make it easier and more routine for you to keep customers abreast of the latest news about your services and your business.

Why is a system useful for me?

A customer management system can be a really great addition to your business as a sports or fitness professional. It can be particularly useful if you find that you have lots of customers trying your services, and you want to make sure that you keep in touch with them on a regular basis. Remember that somebody who has already tried your business is more likely to think about coming back to you again in the future when the need arises. For this reason, you need to stay in touch with past and present students on a regular basis. A customer management system will help make it easier for you to do this.

You can use the system to store all of your customer contact information and also any specific information about them and their preferences. You can collect email information, and it should enable you to send out bulk email to your customers and keep track of who has received what. Without such a system in place, it can become very difficult to keep in touch with large numbers of customers. Therefore, a system such as this enables you to avoid losing the contact information of your customers and creates a way in which you can keep track of who both your current and your past customers are.

Customer management systems may also enable you to keep track of who has clicked on links within your newsletter or your email. This all depends on how the system is designed. Tracking information can be useful to give you a sense of how valuable and successful your electronic marketing efforts are. Without it, you may not get any form of feedback on the material that you send out. You should also be able to use such systems to send out questionnaires to get feedback on how your customers are finding your services.

How can I set up a system?

Generally speaking, the ways to set up a customer management system are:

- **Create one in a spreadsheet**
- **Purchase an off-the-shelf system**
- **Develop your own system**

If you are not sure whether you want to invest a lot of time and money in such a system, you could consider setting one up in a spreadsheet yourself. Alternatively, you could look into whether you can purchase an offline or online version of management system software. If you have your website hosted professionally, you may want to see whether your provider offers any customer management systems that would be suitable for your business.

What do I need to do to maintain a system?

Unfortunately, just having a system itself is only half the work. When you set the system up, you will then also need to fill it with the appropriate information and ensure that you continue to update this data within the system over time. For example, you will need to add the information on new customers and you may decide to archive that on other customers after a certain time period. It may be worthwhile documenting how you intend to manage the information within the system. In this way, you do not have to keep everything in your head. It will also give you the opportunity of being able to ask other people to help you from time to time.

Table 12.5: Using customer management systems

Description	A method of handling your customer information and contact details.
Why it works for sports and fitness businesses	As your business grows, you will end up handling lots of customers, so having a system in place for managing your contact with them will enable you to provide consistent and relevant information.
Cost	Varies depending on the sophistication of the system.
Advantages	Puts a system and process in place for managing all of your customer information and interaction.
Disadvantages	Requires updating regularly.

Using membership management systems

Membership management systems are slightly different from customer management systems. Some may enable you to do all the things that a customer management system can do and some will be completely bespoke membership management tools. The idea is that a membership management tool can help you to manage your active students and also their membership fees, dates, renewal reminders and so on. It should also be able to prepare reports for you that should give you good general information about your customers and perhaps their purchasing habits.

This kind of administrative task can often take up a lot of time and this can all be time that is away from actually doing paid work. If you find that the number of customers with whom you are dealing is more than you can reasonably handle, it can be worthwhile putting in place some kind of system. If you can find a combined customer and membership management system, that should hopefully help to reduce your workload further.

The reason why such a system is good for marketing your business is that it helps you to manage your customer relationship and communications in a more consistent way. Providing such a structured and systematic approach should mean that you can turn the task into something that you can do without taking up too much time or too much thought in the future. Again, you could look into building a simple version in a spreadsheet first and see if that helps you. If it does, you could then look into purchasing an off-the-shelf version of management software.

Table 12.6: Using membership management systems

Description	Putting in place a system and process to manage all of your customer membership information.
Why it works for sports and fitness businesses	Many sports and fitness businesses work on some form of membership basis. You will need to keep track of your customers' training history with you and a membership management system will enable you to do that in a structured way.
Cost	Varies depending on the sophistication of the system.
Advantages	Creates a systematic way for you to manage training and membership information.
Disadvantages	Could be costly and still feel time-consuming.

Summary

Table 12.7 summarises electronic marketing techniques, ranging from using email and mailing lists to using membership management systems. After reviewing these techniques, have a go at exercise 12.1. Make notes on whether you think that a particular marketing technique would be useful to you and how you think you could use it.

Table 12.7: Summary of electronic marketing techniques

Using more advanced computer skills	If you have more advanced computer skills and are comfortable using the Internet, you could give your coaching business a real competitive edge.

Using email and mailing lists	Having a list of all of your customers with whom you can regularly get in touch may cut down on how much information you try to give them during your coaching session. It will also provide you with an additional means of contact.
Developing a website	An Internet presence that markets your business all the time. It can vary from simply providing your contact details to being a full-service electronic shop.
Using electronic newsletters and magazines	Creating a regular way for you to get in touch with your customers outside of your coaching time will enable you to run your business more professionally and also to provide a consistent form of communication to your customers.
Using customer management systems	Having a system and process in place for managing customer information and interaction will make it easier for you to provide a consistent level of service as your customer numbers grow.
Using membership management systems	Having a system and process in place for managing customer training and membership will make it easier for you to manage important information.

Exercise 12.1: Make notes on the usefulness to you of each electronic marketing technique.

MARKETING TECHNIQUE	YOUR NOTES
Using email and mailing lists	
Developing a website	
Using electronic newsletters and magazines	
Using customer management systems	
Using membership management systems	

PART III
CREATING YOUR MARKETING PLAN

CHAPTER 13
PREPARING YOUR TAILOR-MADE MARKETING PLAN

Having spent time putting together descriptions of your business, products and services in part I of this book and then having reviewed which marketing techniques you want to try out in part II, it is now time to put together a manageable marketing plan. Remember that, if the plan is not realistic, you won't be able to implement it easily.

As you worked through part II, you completed exercise 8.1 in which you collected your thoughts on which marketing activities would be relevant for each of your products and services. You should use that information in this chapter too. To kick off the development of your marketing plan, start by listing in exercise 13.1 which marketing techniques you would like to try in the first year. Ideally you want to pick at least six items. You may wish to also list some extra ones to try in case you run into any trouble with the ones that you have picked. You may already have some marketing techniques in place in some form or other and may decide that you would like to work on developing or improving them. You can add them to the list too.

Once you have completed exercise 13.1, you should hopefully have a feel for where you think there might be weaknesses in how well you are promoting each of your items. As you work your way through the remainder of this book and develop your marketing plan, you should review this table again and check that you are making the most of the promotional activities that you have decided to try.

Exercise 13.1: List the marketing techniques that you would like to try or build on in the next year in order of priority. Next to each of the marketing techniques that you have chosen, make some notes to explain why you think it is a good one to try for your business. This will be a helpful reminder when you come to putting your plan into action.

PRIORITY	MARKETING TECHNIQUE	REASON FOR SELECTION
1.		
2.		
3.		
4.		
5.		
6.		
7.		
8.		
9.		
10.		

Planning

This was covered in chapter 6 and now we take a look at your annual programme again while trying to put together your marketing plan. If you have a sports or fitness schedule that is planned well in advance, including all the bookings for venue and equipment orders, this can make marketing all of your activities far easier. However, if you work alone and tend to take a more ad hoc approach to managing your business, you may well find it more difficult to get your head around how marketing will help you. Try exercise 13.2 to gain some insight into your current situation.

Exercise 13.2: Answer the following questions about the current way in which you work.

QUESTION	YOUR ANSWER
Do you arrange your venue bookings at least a year in advance?	
Do you know exactly what dates and times you are planning to coach in the next year?	
Do you know exactly which courses you are planning to run in the next year?	
Do you have all of this information in a calendar?	
Have you decided on your pricing structure for the next year?	
Have you decided on what equipment you will offer in the next year and how often you will be looking to collect orders?	
Do you know the number of people you need to book into a course for you to be happy for it to go ahead?	

If you have answered positively to all of these questions, it looks like you are in great shape to have your marketing efforts work hard for you and maximise their chances of delivering great results. If, as you read the list, you find that there are a number of things on it that you have not yet thought about, hopefully you will start to see why having an organised plan for your activities can help you to market your business effectively. You may look at this list and decide that perhaps it is worthwhile spending a little time getting some things organised before you attempt marketing. The more you know, the better the job you will be able to do in making the most of your marketing.

Before you put together your marketing plan, it can be useful to have a good idea about the kinds of activity that you are going to be doing in the coming year. You can create a marketing plan without this, but it may just look like a list of activities rather than a real plan. The reason why planning is good is that you take away some of the work in advance. Let's look at the simple example of running courses that are booked by the quarter. If you have your programme ready in advance, you can focus all of your efforts throughout the year on just executing your marketing plan at the right time. You will want to promote your courses well in advance so that you stand the best chance of finding the largest possible number of customers.

Advance planning also means that you are making your programme visible to your customers, so that they can make decisions around their own schedule as to what they can fit in and when they might like to start. Without such a framework, you could be losing business. Some training businesses have adopted this method and found that they had customers booking a place sometimes 12 to 18 months in advance of the course start date.

Given that having an annual programme makes sense and should make your life easier, how can you go about developing one? Perhaps you are looking to arrange classes and courses yourself. You'll need to put together a realistic programme that you could try for the next year. For example, if you are already teaching a regular class two evenings a week, jumping to a class every single evening may be a bit too much. However, you may want to consider changing your regular classes into monthly or quarterly courses that you could market and that people could book into in advance. If you are going to hold a number of different types of regular class, you'll want to make sure that you have everything in place to guarantee that you can market your services and products. You'll need to know:

- **which venue to book, how much it costs and what the cancellation charges are**
- **where the venue for the classes is located**
- **what the content of the classes will be**

- **how much to charge for classes**
- **who your target market is for each course or class type**

Being well organised in advance should mean that during the year you can totally focus on marketing and generating new customers to fill the classes and courses that you have already planned. Having to plan the classes as you go along in the year and market them can be incredibly hard work, and for this reason you may well struggle to make them successful.

Timing

Now that you have an idea of what to put in your annual plan, you can start thinking about what are the best methods for promoting each of the activities and what are the best lead times for getting the promotion started.

Case study: Building on a martial arts coaching plan
Let's say that the annual programme includes:

- **Regular classes held each weekday evening**
- **A monthly rolling programme of taster classes**
- **Quarterly premium courses**
- **A quarterly examination of the students to grade them to the next coloured belt**
- **An annual internal competition held at the end of the year**

From this plan you can see that there is a whole host of activities. Some of them are directly aimed at existing customers and others at new ones, and there are even some that are aimed at both.

Ideally, you would want to promote your entire programme a year in advance. If you have a website, this is an excellent place to ensure that full details of all of your courses, classes and products are available. You can then use various other marketing methods to supplement and direct people to your website. You can also use your newsletters or your email marketing programme to draw attention to upcoming events. Your leaflets and brochures could be specific to particular courses or class types that you run. Have a go at putting together lead times for promoting your activities in exercise 13.3.

Exercise 13.3: List the key elements of your programme. Then, for each product and service item, identify your target audience and how far in advance it makes sense for you to start promoting that activity.

TIMING FOR PROMOTION										
TARGET AUDIENCE										
ITEM										

Bringing it all together

Now that you have prepared your list of items that you need to promote and the marketing activities that you wish to try, you can start thinking about how it will all work together. This may seem like quite a lot to think about, but, once you get in the swing of running your marketing programme, it'll start to get easier.

If you have decided to create a website or a brochure that contains all the information on everything you offer, you need to ensure that all of your other marketing material draws your customers towards that more detailed medium. For example, your posters and leaflets may contain only brief information designed to hook your customers. Some people may like to find out more about your business and your services before they feel comfortable enough to get in touch or to come along for some training. For this reason, it can be useful to direct them to your website for more information. The more you can make all of your marketing work together, the easier it should be for you to present yourself professionally, to reduce your workload and to generate a steady stream of new customers.

Drawing up your marketing plan

Once you know which services you are going to run in the next year and which marketing activities you want to try, and you are beginning to think about how it will all work together, that is an excellent time to have a go at drawing up your marketing plan.

Your annual coaching programme

An example of an annual coaching programme is given in table 13.1. After looking at this, use the template in exercise 13.4 to create the latest version of what your annual coaching programme looks like.

Table 13.1: Example of an annual coaching programme

ACTIVITY	JAN	FEB	MAR	APR	MAY	JUN	JUL	AUG	SEP	OCT	NOV	DEC
Regular weekly classes	◆											◆
Quarterly courses	◆		◆	◆		◆	◆		◆	◆		◆
Taster sessions	◆	◆	◆	◆	◆	◆	◆	◆	◆	◆	◆	◆
Private tuition						◆				◆		
Demonstrations	◆			◆			◆			◆		
Specialised workshops		◆		◆		◆		◆		◆		◆
Internal competition												◆
External competitions			◆							◆		

143

Exercise 13.4: Create your annual coaching programme. List your events down the left-hand side of the plan and then draw horizontal lines to map out the duration of each of the activities. Any one-off events, for example competitions, can be represented by a small diamond for that milestone.

ACTIVITY	JAN	FEB	MAR	APR	MAY	JUN	JUL	AUG	SEP	OCT	NOV	DEC

Your annual marketing plan

An example of an annual marketing plan is given in table 13.2. After looking at this, use the template in exercise 13.5 to create the latest version of what your annual marketing plan looks like.

Table 13.2: Example of an annual marketing plan

ACTIVITY	JAN	FEB	MAR	APR	MAY	JUN	JUL	AUG	SEP	OCT	NOV	DEC
Develop marketing materials	◆											◆
Website updated with full annual coaching programme	◆											
Replenish posters and leaflets at all venues	◆											◆
Promote quarterly courses with current students	◆			◆			◆			◆		
Prepare material for taster sessions	◆											
Promote private tuition on the website	◆											
Promote demonstrations with current students	◆			◆			◆			◆		
Promote courses with current students		◆		◆		◆		◆		◆		◆
Promote internal and external competitions	◆											◆
Draw up marketing plan for following year										◆		

145

Exercise 13.5: Create your annual marketing plan. Use your annual coaching programme when thinking about the timing of your marketing activities. List the marketing techniques down the left-hand side of the page and then draw horizontal lines to map out the duration of each of the activities. Any one-off events can be represented by a small diamond for that milestone.

ACTIVITY	JAN	FEB	MAR	APR	MAY	JUN	JUL	AUG	SEP	OCT	NOV	DEC

Your monthly marketing plan

You might find that you would like to underpin your annual plan with a more detailed monthly version. Indeed, if many of the activities that you are planning are likely to be repeated on a monthly basis, you may find a monthly plan useful. Have a go at creating a monthly marketing plan in exercise 13.6. If you don't currently have a repeated monthly activity, try to think of something you could offer in the future.

Exercise 13.6: Create your monthly marketing plan. List the marketing techniques down the left-hand side of the page and then draw horizontal lines to map out the duration of each of the activities. Any one-off events can be represented by a small diamond for that milestone.

WEEK 4								
WEEK 3								
WEEK 2								
WEEK 1								
ACTIVITY								

Your weekly marketing plan

You might find that you would like to underpin your monthly plan with a more detailed weekly plan. Indeed, if many of the activities that you are planning are likely to be repeated on a weekly basis, you may find a weekly plan useful. Have a go at creating a weekly marketing plan in exercise 13.7. If you don't currently have a repeated weekly activity, try to think of something you could offer in the future.

Exercise 13.7: Create your weekly marketing plan. List the marketing techniques down the left-hand side of the page and then draw horizontal lines to map out the duration of each of the activities. Any one-off events can be represented by a small diamond for that milestone.

ACTIVITY	MON	TUE	WED	THU	FRI	SAT	SUN

Review before putting your marketing plan into action

Once you have prepared your marketing plan, you should look at it as a whole and ensure that you have been realistic about when you will be able to do things and how often, and also how long they are likely to take you. Don't create an overambitious plan that sets you up for not being able to meet it at all. Also, take a look at your plan. Does it look like you have planned all the really big activities in a certain part of the year? Is it possible to spread things out a bit more to give yourself the best chance of being able to achieve them?

Implementing your marketing plan

As you start implementing your plan, you will begin to get a sense of what forms of marketing are working for you and also what you are comfortable doing yourself. If you find that some things you try don't work, you can substitute something else in their place.

Use your plan to give you direction throughout the year. You can then relax in the knowledge that, when you first put the plan together, you had a long-term view in mind, and now that you are in the process of delivery, you can focus on making that as successful as possible. Tick off the activities on your plan as you complete them – this will give you a great sense of achievement. This is especially true if, when you get to the end of the year and start thinking about putting together the plan for the following year, you see all the activities that you have already successfully completed.

You may come up with new ideas or feel that some of your initial ideas no longer make sense. That's fine. You don't have to stick to the very first version of your marketing plan. It is *your* plan and you should update and modify it as much as you need to as you learn more and develop your marketing skills. The very first marketing plan is the hardest but you'll have something to start from for the next one.

CHAPTER 14
MEASURING EFFECTIVENESS

Once you have settled into accepting marketing as a normal and everyday part of your business, you may feel that you want to start taking a more formalised approach to measuring the effectiveness of your efforts. You probably already have a good sense of what works and what doesn't. However, as you grow your business and get busier and busier, you need to ensure that whatever time and effort you have available for marketing is maximised through effective use. You may find that a number of techniques that you have tried were successful and so you will continue to use them. Over time, you can keep adding more marketing activities to your plan. However, at some point you may want to step back and try to make things more manageable. How will you decide what to continue and what to stop so that you make room to try something new? You may find that things are successful or disappointing to various degrees. Even the marketing activities that don't work out won't be a complete failure, because you will have learnt quite a lot in the process. And you will be in a better position to assess under what conditions a certain type of marketing may work for you in the future.

Tracking performance

Setting up performance indicators and ways to measure whether an activity was successful can be really useful if they are applied in the right way. If you run short on time in the future, you can then focus your activities on the areas that you know bring in the best results for you. For each of your marketing activities you can identify ways in which you can measure how effective it is. For example, you can ask:

- **How many customers did your leaflets direct to your business within one month of their distribution?**
- **How many enquiries were generated within a certain time period?**
- **How many of those customers came to at least three classes?**
- **How many enquiries, and customers generated, resulted from word-of-mouth referrals within a certain time period?**
- **How much effort does a particular marketing activity involve?**

Hopefully you can see that these questions focus on collecting numerical information. You can collect this kind of data for each marketing activity that you do. You should identify what are the important and relevant questions for your business and answer them for each activity. This process should give you an excellent indication of which of your marketing activities are working the hardest for you. An example of measuring the effectiveness of marketing activities is given in table 14.1. After looking at this, use the template in exercise 14.1 for noting how you can measure the effectiveness of your marketing activities.

Table 14.1: Example of measuring the effectiveness of marketing activities

MARKETING ACTIVITY	MEASURES	RESULTS	YOUR COMMENTS
Website	Target of 5 new customers a month	Total of 5 customers on average achieved this year	Need to increase visitors to the website and to look into ways in which to achieve this
Leaflets	Target of 10 new customers a month	Total of 15 customers on average achieved this year	Need to look into additional places to distribute leaflets
Newspaper advertising	Target of 10 customers per advertisement	Only 1 customer on average per campaign	Need to consider dropping this expensive marketing or to find a more effective way of putting together the advertisement

Exercise 14.1: Measuring the effectiveness of your marketing activities. Write down each of your marketing activities, identify relevant measures of effectiveness for that activity and track the results based on your set targets. Add any additional observations in the final column.

MARKETING ACTIVITY	MEASURES	RESULTS	YOUR COMMENTS

Tracking costs

Another thing that is very easy to lose sight of is how much it costs you to do each marketing activity. This is not just a matter of money, but also how much time and energy it takes out of you. For example, designing and printing leaflets yourself and then also doing the door-to-door distribution yourself is very hard work. Even though you may manage to keep the costs down by personally doing a lot of work, it can take a lot out of you and you need to make sure that it's really worth it. An example of measuring the cost of marketing activities is given in table 14.2. After looking at this, use the template in exercise 14.2 for noting the costs of your marketing activities.

Table 14.2: Example of measuring the cost of marketing activities

MARKETING ACTIVITY	MONEY	TIME	ENERGY	YOUR COMMENTS
Website	£200 per year for hosting	40 hours per year for updating	1 week of work required and at least 1 week of upfront planning	Need to look into ways in which to reduce the hosting costs and the time taken for updating
Leaflets	£500 per year for printing	4 hours a year for updating material	60 hours per year for distribution	• Really tiring and feels inefficient to distribute • Need to find cheaper printing options and also less intensive ways of distribution
Newspaper advertising	£300 per advertisement	4 hours per advertisement	Distribution taken care of by the newspaper	Need to find ways of negotiating the price down or to partner up with another business to get better pricing

Exercise 14.2: Measuring the cost of your marketing activities. Write down each of your marketing activities and note the amount of money, time and energy that each requires. Add any additional observations in the final column.

MARKETING ACTIVITY	MONEY	TIME	ENERGY	YOUR COMMENTS

Looking at your results in exercise 14.2, together with those you obtained for measuring the effectiveness of your marketing activities in exercise 14.1, should help you to start seeing what works for you personally and for your business. Remember that any time and energy that you spend on marketing is potentially time away from fee-paying clients. Be careful not to waste your time on any marketing that doesn't work for you.

CHAPTER 15
MANAGING CUSTOMER SERVICE

Now that you have a steady stream of new customers, you may want to think about putting in place processes that will help you to retain them. Remember that you can go to quite a lot of effort to get your customers in the first place, so once you have them you want to make sure that you do your best to keep hold of them. The way to do this is through customer service. Even if you are just a one-person business, it does not mean that customer service is not important. In fact, customer service is even more important for you. Since you are effectively your business, you will need to ensure that you manage your customer relationships well, so that your customers feel happy to continue with you.

The importance of customer service

A coaching business is a very personal one. You will come into contact with your customers often, and so customer service and customer relationship management are essential for you to retain your customers. Obviously, you should treat your customers well and fairly, and with respect. But you should also bear in mind the following:

- **How do you collect customer feedback?**
- **If you do collect customer feedback, do you act on it promptly and effectively?**
- **How do you handle negative feedback?**
- **Do you ask your students for their input on what other services or products you could offer?**
- **Are you happy to give a refund or a free lesson if there is a problem?**

Handling complaints well is an excellent way to build customer loyalty. If you can show that you take feedback seriously and that you are willing to act decisively, people will respect you for that. In exercise 15.1, make a list of your current mechanisms for receiving feedback, along with any ideas that you have for improving them.

Exercise 15.1 (opposite): List the different ways in which customers give you feedback. In the next column, note any ideas that you have on how you could make it easier for people to give you feedback, or how you could create a process by which people have a way to send you feedback.

CURRENT FEEDBACK MECHANISMS	IDEAS FOR HOW YOU COULD IMPROVE THEM

As a coach you will often be in a position where you also come into contact with your customers' family and friends. You should ensure that you treat them just as fairly and with respect. You are judged not only on how you respond to your students, but also on how you deal with other people, and that can directly impact your business relationship with your customer.

If you have already put in place a customer management system, that should make things a little easier for you to keep track of. You should ensure that your system is updated regularly with all the relevant information. Remember that your system is only as good as the information that you put in it.

Preparing a customer service plan

Once you have established your business, customer service and customer retention can become more important. To this extent, you may even wish to consider putting together a customer service action plan. You might want to include schemes such as:

- **Putting in place a feedback mechanism**
- **Designing and distributing questionnaires at the end of courses**
- **Setting up a complaints handling procedure and mechanism for refunds or goodwill**

An example of a customer service plan is given in table 15.1. After looking at this, use the template in exercise 15.2 for drawing up your customer service plan.

Table 15.1: Example of a customer service plan

ACTIVITY	JAN	FEB	MAR	APR	MAY	JUN	JUL	AUG	SEP	OCT	NOV	DEC
Customer information management	Understand and implement data protection legislation as it applies to this business (JAN–MAR)					Collect customer contact information (MAR–JUN)						Study customer information to develop business and marketing efforts (DEC)
							Keep records of customer transactions and renewals (JUL–AUG)					
							Automate renewals notification (AUG–OCT)					
Collecting customer feedback	Develop and implement a questionnaire for collecting feedback (JAN–JUL)											
				Start to implement changes based on customer feedback (FEB–APR)								
					Link customer feedback into the customer information management system (MAY–JUN)							
					Develop and implement electronic questionnaires for collecting feedback (JUN–OCT)							Study customer feedback to develop business and marketing efforts (DEC)

Exercise 15.2: Your customer service plan. List the activity categories down the left-hand side of the page. Then draw horizontal lines to map out the duration of the activities.

ACTIVITY	JAN	FEB	MAR	APR	MAY	JUN	JUL	AUG	SEP	OCT	NOV	DEC

It is even better if you can come up with ways in which to incorporate your customer service and relationship management within the marketing methods that you already have in place. For example:

- **If you have a website, you could add a feedback form or expressly request that feedback information be emailed to you.**
- **If you already hand out leaflets or brochures to students, you could include a short questionnaire or a note to collect customer feedback.**
- **If you send out an electronic newsletter, you could mention that you are happy to receive customer feedback, and you could consider doing online or email surveys.**

If you do put in place mechanisms by which to receive feedback, make sure that you have some way of dealing with it. If you have a lot of customers whom you are dealing with on your own, the more structured your business, the easier it should be for you to focus on operation. The key is to make any processes that you do put in place as simple and effortless as possible. The more complicated you make things, the harder it will be for you to maintain the same level of customer service over time. Simple and effective is what you want to aim for.

CHAPTER 16
THE ONGOING MARKETING PROCESS

Having gone through the exercise of creating and implementing a marketing plan, you probably feel that your knowledge of both your business and your customers has really improved. Based on this improved knowledge, you perhaps are starting to come up with ideas for new things to try both within your business and within the marketing of your services. It is important to review the type of information that you pulled together in part I of this book. A good time to do a quick review and see if you need to update any of that information is when you are starting to bring together your next marketing plan. Each year you should consider trying a new service or try marketing what you do in a new way.

Over time you may find that the templates in this book are useful in terms of helping you to focus on the important aspects of your business. You could keep copies of the plans and information that you collect: these will build up a picture of how both you and your business are developing and help you to start thinking about where you might like your business to go in the future.

Your five-year plan

A lot of the plans in this book are annual plans, but there is no reason why you can't start to prepare a longer-term plan that highlights your ambitions for your business. You will hopefully find that this helps to guide both your service offering and your marketing in a more focused way, leading to a coordinated approach to achieving success over a much longer term. Have a look at the example of a five-year marketing plan in table 16.1. Now create your own five-year marketing plan in exercise 16.1.

Table 16.1: Example of a five-year marketing plan

ACTIVITY	YEAR 1	YEAR 2	YEAR 3	YEAR 4	YEAR 5
Develop website	One-page website with basic details only	Add book reviews and equipment list	Add online shop for equipment	Add online booking form for courses	Add online payment facility for courses
Develop newsletter	Establish a leaflet-style quarterly news-letter	Post newsletter onto website each quarter including back issues	Develop a customer email list	Switch to electronic-style newsletter	Develop tracking capability in the electronic newsletter
Develop instructional booklets	Develop a one-page information sheet for students	Develop single sheet into a series of infor-mation sheets	Compile into a print-at-home booklet	Develop a series of booklets	Compile booklets into a bound book

Exercise 16.1: Your five-year marketing plan. List the activities down the left-hand side of the page. Then add your goal for each year in the following columns.

ACTIVITY	YEAR 1	YEAR 2	YEAR 3	YEAR 4	YEAR 5

FURTHER READING

Burg, B., *Endless Referrals*, McGraw-Hill (2006).

Edwards, P., Edwards, S. and Clampitt Douglas, L., *Getting Business to Come to You*, J. P. Tarcher (1998).

Harding, F., *Cross-Selling Success*, Adams Media Corporation (2002).

Mills, H., *The Rainmaker's Toolkit*, Amacom (2004).

Silbiger, S., *The Ten-Day MBA*, William Morrow & Co (1993).

INDEX

Also available from A&C Black Publishers:

Fitness Professionals: The Advanced Fitness Instructor's Handbook
by **Morc Coulson and David Archer**

Following on from *The Fitness Instructor's Handbook*, this book covers the National Occupational Standards and the Qualifications framework for Level 3 and Level 4 Instructors teaching Exercise and Fitness – required to teach one-on-one, and the standard that gyms are increasingly expecting staff to attain.

The Complete Guide to Sport Motivation
by **Ken Hodge**

This practical handbook tells you everything you need to achieve excellence in sport, treating the mind as an essential part of training. It covers psychological skills training; anxiety and peak performance; self-confidence, motivation and mental toughness; coping with pressure; communication and team-building; concentration; psychological rehabilitation from injury; goal-setting; planning a total training programme.

The Personal Trainer's Handbook
by **Rebecca Weissbort**

A one-stop practical reference guide to the day-to-day running of a personal training business, covering:

- essential business skills – how to target your market, insurance, finances, marketing
- personal development – fitness and safety, managing the work/life balance
- how to deal with clients – the first meeting, creating the right programme, typical client groups, considerations for special client groups

Available from all good bookshops or online. For more details on these and other A&C Black sport and fitness titles, please go to www.acblack.com.